INTERNATIONAL DEVELOPMENT IN FOCUS

Blue Routes for a New Era

Developing Inland Waterways Transportation in China

BERNARD ARITUA, LU CHENG, RICHARD VAN LIERE, AND HARRIE DE LEIJER

WORLD BANK GROUP

© 2020 International Bank for Reconstruction and Development / The World Bank
1818 H Street NW, Washington, DC 20433
Telephone: 202-473-1000; Internet: www.worldbank.org

Some rights reserved

1 2 3 4 23 22 21 20

Books in this series are published to communicate the results of Bank research, analysis, and operational experience with the least possible delay. The extent of language editing varies from book to book.

This work is a product of the staff of The World Bank with external contributions. The findings, interpretations, and conclusions expressed in this work do not necessarily reflect the views of The World Bank, its Board of Executive Directors, or the governments they represent. The World Bank does not guarantee the accuracy of the data included in this work. The boundaries, colors, denominations, and other information shown on any map in this work do not imply any judgment on the part of The World Bank concerning the legal status of any territory or the endorsement or acceptance of such boundaries.

Nothing herein shall constitute or be considered to be a limitation upon or waiver of the privileges and immunities of The World Bank, all of which are specifically reserved.

Rights and Permissions

This work is available under the Creative Commons Attribution 3.0 IGO license (CC BY 3.0 IGO) http://creativecommons.org/licenses/by/3.0/igo. Under the Creative Commons Attribution license, you are free to copy, distribute, transmit, and adapt this work, including for commercial purposes, under the following conditions:

Attribution—Please cite the work as follows: Aritua, Bernard, Lu Cheng, Richard van Liere, and Harrie de Leijer. 2020. *Blue Routes for a New Era: Developing Inland Waterways Transportation in China.* International Development in Focus. Washington, DC: World Bank. doi:10.1596/978-1-4648-1584-3. License: Creative Commons Attribution CC BY 3.0 IGO

Translations—If you create a translation of this work, please add the following disclaimer along with the attribution: *This translation was not created by The World Bank and should not be considered an official World Bank translation. The World Bank shall not be liable for any content or error in this translation.*

Adaptations—If you create an adaptation of this work, please add the following disclaimer along with the attribution: *This is an adaptation of an original work by The World Bank. Views and opinions expressed in the adaptation are the sole responsibility of the author or authors of the adaptation and are not endorsed by The World Bank.*

Third-party content—The World Bank does not necessarily own each component of the content contained within the work. The World Bank therefore does not warrant that the use of any third-party-owned individual component or part contained in the work will not infringe on the rights of those third parties. The risk of claims resulting from such infringement rests solely with you. If you wish to re-use a component of the work, it is your responsibility to determine whether permission is needed for that re-use and to obtain permission from the copyright owner. Examples of components can include, but are not limited to, tables, figures, or images.

All queries on rights and licenses should be addressed to World Bank Publications, The World Bank Group, 1818 H Street NW, Washington, DC 20433, USA; e-mail: pubrights@worldbank.org.

ISBN: 978-1-4648-1584-3

DOI: 10.1596/978-1-4648-1584-3
Cover photo: © Wenqiao Hu. Grand Canal at Huzhou. Used with permission; further permission required for reuse.
Cover design: Debra Naylor / Naylor Design Inc.

Contents

Figures

Maps

Photos

Tables

Foreword

In 2018, China celebrated the 40th anniversary of its "reform and opening up." During this 40-year period of rapid economic growth and poverty reduction, more than 800 million people—equivalent to about 75 percent of the population of Africa— have been lifted out of poverty, and China has progressed from one of the poorest nations to an upper-middle-income country. China's share of global gross domestic product (GDP) increased from 1.8 percent in 1980 to about 18.7 percent in 2018 and national GDP expanded 25-fold. The details of how this development outcome was achieved are evolving. Overall, however, the reforms that led to the dramatic growth included experimentation in policy and institutional design, along with the gradual opening of the economy to market forces, foreign direct investment, and targeted initiatives. The transport sector, as the backbone of the drivers of growth, is an important part of China's growth story. During the period of rapid growth, China also developed its transport system and infrastructure. Since 1990, China has added more than 120,000 kilometers of railways, 130,000 kilometers of expressways, 3 million kilometers of roads, and 127,000 kilometers of navigable inland waterways.

The World Bank has been a partner with China on this journey. Over the past three decades, the World Bank has approved more than 110 transportation projects in China, with a total investment of $19 billion. The World Bank has also been a knowledge partner, producing more than 15 targeted studies captured in the *China Transport Topics* series. The World Bank and China's Ministry of Transport have jointly developed the Transport Transformation and Innovation Knowledge Platform (TransFORM) program—a flagship knowledge platform to share Chinese and international transport experiences and facilitate learning within China and other World Bank client countries. What can other countries learn from China's success? Although China's socioeconomic context is different from that of many countries, relevant practices and experience may be distilled for emerging economies looking for sustainable solutions to transport development challenges. Through TransFORM, the World Bank is analyzing China's experience in five areas of transport—high-speed rail, highways, urban transport, ports, and inland waterways—to identify lessons that are transferrable from China to other emerging economies. Its first report was on high-speed rail development; this report on inland waterway transport is the second in the series.

China's inland waterway transport (IWT) system went from carrying less than 150 million tons of cargo in 1978 to carrying 3.74 billion tons of cargo in 2018—six times more than either the European Union or the United States. China now has the busiest IWT system in the world. China's leadership in IWT development started with years of investment in infrastructure that transformed low-grade waterways into high-grade ones, which allowed larger vessels to use the waterways and resulted in higher transport efficiency and lower cost. China invested heavily in upgrading the physical infrastructure and development of skills and technical know-how. To date, there are 127,000 kilometers of inland waterways with high-quality navigability and a good safety record. Most of the IWT projects in China were completed in a timely manner during the period of rapid development in which China also adopted or developed internationally recognized technical innovations for river classification, vessel replacement, navigation technology, and environmental protection.

Forty years ago, IWT in China had nearly lost its significance—the development of highways and rail transportation had become a priority for China, and IWT was not considered a critical part of a modern transportation system. Today, many countries face similar situations. Although endowed with inland waterways, the transportation of goods and people by waterways does not feature in policy decisions. The reform process and IWT development in China turned the dormant IWT sector into a vibrant mode of transport, greatly contributing to the development of areas along riverbanks and turning waterways and their hinterlands into economic corridors. What China achieved can be informative; however, the "how" and "why" of China's improvements to inland waterways for transportation is especially relevant and provides valuable lessons for other countries.

Moreover, the Chinese IWT system is still developing; ongoing innovations are improving the efficiency, sustainability, and safety of the system. Cooperation with other countries is helping produce an even better IWT system. What are the areas in which China's IWT could develop even further? This report also discusses comparisons, case studies, examples, and practices from across the world and presents opportunities to further improve the IWT system in China and globally.

Martin Raiser
Country Director, China, Mongolia, and Korea,
World Bank Group

Fei Weijun
President, China Waterborne Transport Research Institute,
China

Vivien Foster
Chief Economist, Infrastructure Practice Group,
World Bank Group

Acknowledgments

This report is an output of the Transport Global Practice of the World Bank Group. It was prepared by Bernard Aritua, Lu Cheng, Richard van Liere, and Harrie de Leijer. The primary research that underpins this report was undertaken by the China Waterborne Transport Research Institute (WTI). The authors are grateful to researchers from WTI: Jia Dashan, Wu Jialu, Wang Bin, Chen Yihao, Yu Xiujuan, Ning Tao, Cai Ouchen, and Zhang Zhehui. The report also benefited from contributions by WTI staff: Ma Yanyan, Sun Ting, Guo Yanchen, Yang Yahe, Yu Yuanyuan, and Hu Yiyi. The authors are thankful for the support from Xu Honglei, Wang Renjie, and Yanyan from the China Transport Planning and Research Institute.

The authors acknowledge the excellent discussions and feedback from various policy makers and officials from public organizations responsible for inland waterway transportation in various countries. We are grateful to experts from the following organizations for sharing their experience and insights and providing data: Inland Waterways Authority of India (IWAI), Central Commission for Navigation on the Rhine (CCNR), United Nations Economic Commission for Europe (UNECE), US Army Corps of Engineers (USACE), World Association for Waterborne Transport Infrastructure (PIANC), Danube Commission (DC), Ministry of Infrastructure and Water Management and Rijkswaterstaat of the Netherlands, United Nations Economic and Social Commission for Asia and the Pacific (UNESCAP), Universidad del Norte Barranquilla, Instituto Nacional del Agua Argentina (INA), Agência Nacional de Transportes Aquaviários Brazil (Antaq), Agência Nacional de Transportes Terrestres Brazil (ANTT), and ViaDonau.

The report benefited from valuable expert advice received from peer reviewers: Arnab Bandyopadhyay, Luis C. Blancas Mendivil, Charles Kunaka, Edwin Lock, James Wang, and Hans van der Werf. Special thanks to Huijing Deng for providing analytical support. The authors are grateful to Martin Raiser, Country Director for China, Mongolia, and the Republic of Korea, and Binyam Reja, Transport Global Practice Manager for China and Mongolia, for their guidance and support in preparing this report, and to Vivien Foster, Chief Economist for the Infrastructure Global Practice at the World Bank, for technical review.

The authors also wish to acknowledge various reports and policy documents that have been referred to in the study and referenced in this report.

The authors are grateful to Sara Sultan (Senior Knowledge Management Office) for her advice on publishing and dissemination of the report. Barbara Karni provided editorial support, and Azeb Afework and Zijing Niu provided outstanding operational and administrative support.

Funding for this report was provided by the China–World Bank Group Partnership Facility (CWPF). The objective of the CWPF is to assist member countries of the participating World Bank Group organizations in achieving inclusive and sustainable development. This report is disseminated under the umbrella of TransFORM, the Transport Transformation and Innovation Knowledge Platform, which is jointly convened by the government of China and the World Bank.

About the Authors

Bernard Aritua is a senior infrastructure specialist at the World Bank Group. He has worked in the field of infrastructure development and economic policy for more than 20 years. During this time, he has led and provided technical input on policy analysis, regulation, institutional reform, and the technical design of major highways, railways, inland waterways transportation, freight logistics, and multimodal transport. He has published more than 50 reports, articles in peer-reviewed international journals, and contributed to several international conferences. Prior to joining the World Bank, he worked in both the private and public sectors. He has lived and worked in several countries and regions, including the United Kingdom, Germany, Eastern Europe, Africa, the Middle East, and more recently, India and China. He is a Chartered Engineer with a PhD in Civil Engineering from the University of Leeds, United Kingdom, and is a member of the Chartered Institution of Highways and Transportation and the Institute of Asset Management.

Lu Cheng is a senior researcher at the China Waterborne Transport Research Institute (WTI). He has had more than 20 years of experience in the waterway transport industry, and he is a respected specialist on inland waterway transport, intermodal port management, and logistics. He has led and been involved in many key national and ministerial projects in China's waterway transport industry, focusing on market analysis, policy designing, planning, knowledge exchanging, and training. He has several years of consulting experience in government, public agencies, and private enterprises in China. He is actively involved in research and consulting in the waterway transport and logistics sector for international institutions. To support the development of sustainable transport, he is currently providing support for the Asia-Pacific Economic Cooperation Port Services Network (APSN), in which he has gained considerable experience on knowledge exchange, capacity building, and sustainability promotion programs such as the Green Port Award System.

Harrie de Leijer is a specialist in multimodal transportation with a focus on ports, inland waterways, and hinterland connectivity. He has carried out multimodal transport projects in Europe, Asia, South America, and Africa for international agencies and institutions, governments, and private organizations. He specializes in developing integrated transport master plans that combine elements of infrastructure, markets, institutional organization, supporting systems, and knowledge exchange. For three decades he has actively promoted the use of inland waterways as a transport mode. His inland waterway transport expertise is acknowledged worldwide, and he is frequently asked to participate as an expert in inland waterway transport studies and projects, and he speaks at international conferences, workshops, and seminars. His involvement in Chinese inland waterway transport development started in 1996, and he has been an ongoing participant ever since.

Richard van Liere is a specialist in multimodal transport and port-hinterland connectivity. Over the past decade, he has acquired specific knowledge and experience in the development of inland waterway transport as part of multi-modal transport solutions. In the field of inland waterway transport, he has successfully completed several projects in Europe, Asia, and South America for international financial institutions, national and regional governments, indus-try associations, and private organizations. He has gained experience in sus-tainable inland waterway transport development, looking into topics like: multimodal analysis, corridor development, and modal shift potential; river information services and digitization; integrative development of waterway infrastructure; and various studies related to the greening of inland vessels (after-treatment systems, LNG, electric, hydrogen), with the aim to contribute to a zero-emission transport system by 2050.

Abbreviations

AIS	automatic identification system
CCNR	Central Commission for Navigation of the Rhine
CJHDJ	Yangtze Waterway Bureau
CJHY	Yangtze River Administration of Navigational Affairs
CSC	Changjiang National Shipping Corporation
DC	Danube Commission
DWT	deadweight tons
EU	European Union
GDP	gross domestic product
GNS	good navigation status
GVCs	global value chains
ICPR	International Commission for Protection of the Rhine
ICT	information and communication technology
IPCC	Intergovernmental Panel on Climate Change
IT	information technology
IWT	inland waterway transport
LNG	liquefied natural gas
MoT	Ministry of Transport, China
MWR	Ministry of Water Resources
NAIADES	Navigation and Inland Waterway Action and Development in Europe
NDRC	National Development and Reform Commission
NOx	nitrogen oxides
PIANC	World Association for Waterborne Transport Infrastructure
PM	particulate matter
PPP	public-private partnership
R&D	research and development
RIS	river information services
RoRo	roll-on/roll-off
SMEs	small and medium enterprises
TEN-T	Trans-European Network for Transport

TEU	twenty-foot equivalent unit
TransFORM	Transport Transformation and Innovation Knowledge Platform
USACE	US Army Corps of Engineers
USDOT	US Department of Transportation
WTI	China Waterborne Transport Research Institute
ZJHW	Pearl River Administration of Navigational Affairs

Overview

Many of the world's rivers that used to anchor national freight and associated economic activities no longer do so (for example, the Amazon, the Nile, the Ganges, and the Volga). Today, most of those waterways carry insignificant volumes and numbers of people compared with the past and certainly relative to the size of the countries' economies in which they are located.

The drive for sustainable transportation that meets economic goals while reducing the impact on the environment and society has refocused policy makers' attention on the potential of inland waterway transport (IWT), which has significant advantages over or in combination with other modes in logistics chains. In countries that have developed IWT, it has provided an alternative low-carbon mode for moving people and freight, and its advantage increases with transport distance and cargo volume. In addition to economic advantages, IWT also offers societal benefits, as emissions per ton and ton-kilometer are lower than alternative modes. Also, IWT produces fewer other negative externalities, including accidents and noise, and it is safer for transporting hazardous cargoes. It fits well in modern multimodal supply chains, offering attractive solutions to shippers.

In general, many policy makers readily acknowledge the economic, environmental, and social benefits of IWT. But why do many countries struggle to develop their IWT? One reason is because of the dearth of successful examples of IWT revival. Inland waterway transport in the United States and in Europe is relatively successful and has a long history. But the experience of many emerging countries has been a tale of intensive use followed by total collapse of the IWT sector. However, the combination of societal, economic, and environmental imperatives is motivating a rethinking. China's experience has similarities to what many countries are experiencing and offers valuable insights and lessons for other countries. This report is the result of a retrospective study of IWT in China and it provides insights that fill a global knowledge gap in IWT.

It must be acknowledged upfront that the experience of China is not directly applicable to all countries. The context and governance in China are not typical. Furthermore, the approach to policy making and reform, which consisted of several trial-and-error iterations, may not be suitable for all countries. Nevertheless, the experience of reviving IWT in China is truly unprecedented and could benefit policy makers globally.

SCOPE OF THE REPORT

This report is intended as a quick reference with practical examples and lessons captured in a format to stimulate thinking. It is not intended to be a tool kit or policy guide to be followed outside the context of structured policy making. Also, the examples and case studies are not necessarily to be taken as a panacea. Rather, these should be considered as good examples, and their relevance should be considered in context.

PRIMARY AUDIENCE

The primary audience for the report is policy makers and senior officials in government organizations in emerging economies who are grappling with the challenge of how to revive IWT in their countries. As a result, the report captures the experience of reviving IWT in China in formats that can be used to stimulate discussion, and the orientation and academic detail have been adjusted accordingly. The report was developed on the basis of interactions with and strong demand from relevant public officials involved in IWT in various emerging economies.

This retrospective is also useful for policy makers in China as areas for current and future priorities, and opportunities for international cooperation, are identified.

LESSONS FROM CHINA

China handles the world's largest volume of IWT, totaling 3.74 billion tons in 2018. Besides China, only the European Union and the United States have IWT volumes that exceed 500 million tons a year. Only six waterways in the world have annual volumes of more than 100 million tons. The top three of those waterways are in China—the Yangtze, Pearl, and Grand Canal. The other three of those six waterways are the Rhine, the Mississippi River, and the Mekong.

China's achievements in IWT are notable given how quickly they occurred. For example, container throughput at Yangtze inland ports rose from close to 106,000 twenty-foot equivalent units (TEUs) in 1990 to 19.6 million TEUs in 2018. This change required new port facilities, new vessels, and warehousing for packing and unpacking containers. The government introduced several policies to attract higher-value containerized cargo transport on waterways.

Although the rapid growth of IWT in China is recent, the use of IWT in China has a long history. As is the case in other countries, IWT in China was instrumental in shaping economic development for centuries. However, in the twentieth century, the use of water for irrigation, for potable water, and for power generation became more important and took precedence over transportation. As in other countries, the final blow to IWT was the development of road and rail transport, which were considered more modern than IWT and attracted significant investments.

The reform and innovation process of China's IWT sector turned a dormant sector into a vibrant mode of transport that is once again contributing to the development of areas along riverbanks and turning them into wider economic corridors. In some areas, China faced a unique set of circumstances and institutions that contributed to the revival of IWT; therefore, not all experiences from

China are replicable. However, for many emerging economies that are endowed with inland waterways but for which transportation by waterways has lost its historical role, China's experience provides useful lessons and could offer a basis for informed decisions.

The lessons from China may be grouped into the following five main categories:

- *Strong and sustained support from the highest levels of government coupled with coordinated central planning and support systems are a prerequisite for addressing the multisector and multiuser challenges in reviving IWT.* From early in the reform and opening-up period, the revival of IWT was considered a national priority, and it was kept to the fore by senior policy makers who recognized that efficient IWT was strongly linked to the economic growth of China. The thrust of the strong relationship between economic and social prosperity and transportation along the waterways was highlighted throughout the period of revival. In addition, five-year development plans, in which clear and tangible goals were set by the National Development and Reform Commission, were critical in providing the predictable path for revival. Those plans were implemented with policies and directives and discipline, thereby building confidence in the sector and supply chains. Significantly, the plans were not wish lists; they were achievable goals linked to the overall economic development of main corridors and the nation.

- *Strong institutions with clear roles and responsibilities are needed for coordinated development of inland waterway transport.* The coordination of different parties involved in the development of IWT has been a major factor in the sector's success. Since reform and opening up, the combination of central and regional systems, the distribution of responsibilities at different levels, and joint construction have created a framework for accelerating the development of inland waterway infrastructure and associated elements. As part of the reform process, the central government adopted a clearer policy-making role, and it established river navigation and administrative institutions to take care of navigation along individual waterways. In addition, provinces were given explicit responsibility for funding and maintaining the fairways. This responsibility was backed by regulatory authority to raise financing for implementation. Defined roles and responsibilities have worked well for the development of IWT in China.

- *After several years of noninvestment, public sector funding is inevitable—especially during nascent stages*. When the goal to revive IWT in China was set, the sector had more or less collapsed. As a result, the barriers to entry for operators were high and commercial banks found the sector extremely risky. Thus, from a messaging perspective but also from initial experimentation with funding the sector, the government of China provided the resources not only to develop core infrastructure but also to remove the risk from various aspects, such as vessel replacement and development of inland ports, and thereby encouraged alternative sources of finance. A special and dedicated fund for IWT was set up by the central government; individual provinces were also allowed to propose mechanisms for guarantee schemes and special levies to raise the necessary funding for IWT.

- *The improvement of infrastructure and fairways, the standardization of vessels, and the classification of waterways need to be synchronized.* Unlike many countries that take a piecemeal approach to developing aspects of IWT, China learned early on from experiences in Europe and the United States that all parts of the IWT ecosystem need to be developed in tandem to achieve long-term goals. From improving the infrastructure of the core network and the classification of waterways, to the upgrading of vessels, of navigational aids, human resources, and links between IWT and the hinterland—all aspects were developed in tandem. This synchronization of development is an important lesson: the experience in other countries shows that policy makers do not always give attention to the entire ecosystem; often they will invest in dredging the waterways—which is an important and costly element of IWT—without paying attention to the other elements.

- *Dedicated education and learning institutions for all aspects of IWT are needed to revive the sector*. In addition to investing in infrastructure and related policies, China established a full spectrum of educational institutions related to IWT; it is the only country in the world to have established inland shipping universities. In all other countries, IWT personnel are educated in vocational schools and IWT professions cannot generally achieve academic qualifications in the sector. In addition, China has established many shipping colleges and schools with continuously upgraded curriculum to ensure IWT personnel are qualified in an ever-changing landscape (for example, the modernization of the sector and upgrading of vessels and equipment, the adoption of new technologies, and the handling of hazardous cargoes).

WHAT IS THE OUTLOOK FOR IWT IN CHINA IN THE NEW ERA?

Challenges remain for China's IWT sector: policy makers are grappling with whether new infrastructure should be developed or whether new ways of developing IWT need to be adopted from other countries. Balancing the interests of navigation with other uses of water resources needs to be addressed in an integrated manner that safeguards the interests of different stakeholders. In those areas, international best practices could be useful. In addition, the reality of climate change underscores the potential role of IWT in adaptation and mitigation; much can still be done to improve the environmental performance of IWT in China. Also, rapidly changing technology and concepts of smart shipping, including autonomous shipping, offer huge potential to the sector, but much work needs to be done before IWT can achieve its full potential and harness new technology. The challenges posed by climate change and the opportunities from rapid technological change require international cooperation and coordination.

China's current priorities and its options for further reform and development can be grouped under the following headings:

- *Implementing deeper market reforms and increasing IWT's modal share.* The Chinese economy is at an inflection point—transitioning from an export-led economy to one that is driven by increased productivity and private consumption. This type of economy requires a different transport system and logistics configuration. As a result of this structural change in the economy and rising private consumption, the composition of IWT cargo is slowly changing, as the demand for containers grows and the demand for bulky and low-value materials (such as coal, iron ore, construction materials, and other minerals/low-value commodities) slows. For example, changing environmental policies have led to growing demand for liquefied natural gas and the development of roll-on/roll-off (RoRo) transport. New markets for IWT could develop because of the increase in biomass, urban distribution, e-commerce, and small shipments. Further reforms that focus on the customer and associated logistics services are required for IWT to play an important role in the new economic reality. A "build it and they shall come" approach is not viable in the new economy.

- *Integrating IWT into overall water resources management, planning, and governance.* As is the case in many countries, institutions for waterways were developed with specific sector objectives. However, with their development, aligning competing realities become a challenge. In China, different authorities are responsible for their respective aspects of waterways. The conflicting priorities of these authorities and the institutional gaps between them become evident in times of crisis. A coordination mechanism needs to be established to ensure that they work in concert. For example, during a drought, the inland shipping sector with the local and central agencies will require a minimum water level to guarantee good draft for navigation. Irrigation authorities will need to extract more water to prevent drying/dying crops. Hydropower facilities will want to safeguard a continuous flow of water through their turbines. These interests may conflict; a coordinating mechanism is required to reconcile them. In addition, the wide variations in water levels that are likely because of climate change increase the need for such coordination.

- *Greening IWT and adapting to climate change.* China is devoting increasing attention to the environmental performance of IWT and the adaptation of waterways to climate change. Actively promoting the application of new and clean energy is a priority for the government. To address climate change and to make the sector greener, China needs to tackle several challenges, including controlling emissions from inland vessels; the supervision of marine fuel quality; implementing an environmentally friendly mechanism for reception, transport, and disposal areas of pollutants; promoting sustainable shore power use; conserving energy at ports; greening ports and expanding concepts about working with nature; and smart inland shipping.

- *Improving multimodal connectivity and accelerating technological innovations.* New logistics concepts such as cross-chain control and synchromodality are dramatically changing how goods are moved or processed. Those trends are accelerated by disruptive technologies—such as blockchain, big-data analytics, advanced robotics, and artificial intelligence—which are reshaping end-to-end logistics and will inevitably affect the role of carriers and the decisions of shippers. As an example, global supply chains increasingly involve multiple participants such as manufactures, forwarders, shippers, customs agents, and insurers. Innovations in the application of blockchain technology are helping in dispute resolution by improving administrative efficiency and order tracking. Contract logistic companies or various actors in the supply chains can now track all components on an unchangeable and authentic digital ledger. In many cases, the easy coordination of documents on a shared distributed ledger means that physical paperwork is largely unnecessary. Blockchain ensures trustworthy data transfer and sharing across the transportation and logistic ecosystem because the entire network contributes to data validation. Rapid changes in concepts of logistics and applications of disruptive technology present opportunities for increased efficiency and safety, but they also present challenges. The drive toward intelligent shipping demonstrates the potential in China's IWT sector.

- **Developing human capital for the new era.** The full spectrum of trained professionals, from qualified crew trained in vocational institutions to professionals trained in universities, was critical for the revival of China's IWT sector. At the current point of inflection, as China enters a new era, new challenges are present. Not only is there a shortage of a new generation of IWT professionals, but also technology requires a total rethinking of what those professionals should be.

WHAT ARE THE AREAS FOR CONTINUED INTERNATIONAL COOPERATION IN IWT?

While reviving its IWT sector, China benefited from the experiences of other countries. In addition, international institutions such as the World Bank played an important role in the process by providing knowledge and expertise, financing, and also convening countries with shared interests. Also, international forums and partners have enabled global cooperation that has advanced IWT. In the early years of China's IWT revival, the focus was mainly on infrastructure development, such as waterway regulation and the construction of hydropower-cum-ship-lock complexes. Later, the focus was on support systems for traffic guidance, safety, and waste management. Recently, greening IWT and improving its environmental performance have become priorities. At the same time, logistics projects, such as the development of ports in combination with logistics zones, have been implemented.

Going forward, there is a continued need for international cooperation that focuses on introducing and implementing new philosophies and new technologies that will lead to more sustainable transport systems and to better climate change adaptability on a global scale. No single country can tackle those global challenges by itself. If tackled jointly, the benefits of such actions are also shared globally. Therefore, knowledge exchange in a rapidly changing world is needed and international cooperation should focus on the following priority areas:

- Innovative approaches and concepts for multidisciplinary waterway management and planning, which accelerate climate change adaptation and mitigation
- Research, international cooperation, and coordination on intelligent shipping
- Promotion of modal shift by enhancing the role of small and medium enterprises (SMEs) in the IWT sector
- Research and introduction of technologies for modern, green, and sustainable IWT vessels
- Establishment of a knowledge exchange mechanism and support system for global cooperation

1 Growth of Inland Waterway Transport in China

BENEFITS OF INLAND WATERWAY TRANSPORT

Inland waterway transport (IWT) offers societal benefits; its emissions, energy use, accident rates, and noise per ton and ton-kilometer are lower compared with those of alternative systems. In addition, IWT is the safest way to transport hazardous cargoes, and it helps relieve congestion on roads. When designed appropriately, IWT fits neatly into modern multimodal supply chains, offering attractive solutions to shippers.

The drive for sustainable transportation that meets economic goals while reducing the impact on the environment and society has refocused the attention of policy makers on the potential of IWT, which has significant advantages over or in combination with other modes in logistics supply chains. In countries that have developed IWT, it has provided an alternative low-carbon means for moving people and freight, and its advantage increases with transport distance and cargo volume. In mature IWT systems that are characterized by modern vessels with low energy use and efficient operations, IWT is also cost-effective for shorter distances and smaller shipments. IWT may even be an option for distances of 20–40 kilometers, especially in cases without pre- and end haulage by road (see photo 1.1).

In addition to its economic advantages, IWT also offers societal benefits, as emissions per ton and ton-kilometer are lower alternative modes. Recent European data indicate that IWT's environmental performance per ton-kilometer for a bulk vessel is only 10 percent of that of a truck's for carbon dioxide (CO_2) emission, 13 percent of a truck's for nitrogen oxides (NOx), and 50 percent of a truck's for particulate matter (PM) (CE Delft 2017). Data from the United States indicate that CO_2 emissions per unit turnover of barges are just 8 percent of highway transport's, NOx emissions are 4 percent of highway transport's, and PM emissions are 25 percent of highway transport's (US Environmental Protection Agency 2018).

Locating economic and industrial activities along waterways reduces the cost of IWT. Since the dawn of history, inland waterway transport has been a critical mode for transporting goods and persons and remains an important and integral

PHOTO 1.1
Circumvention of traffic

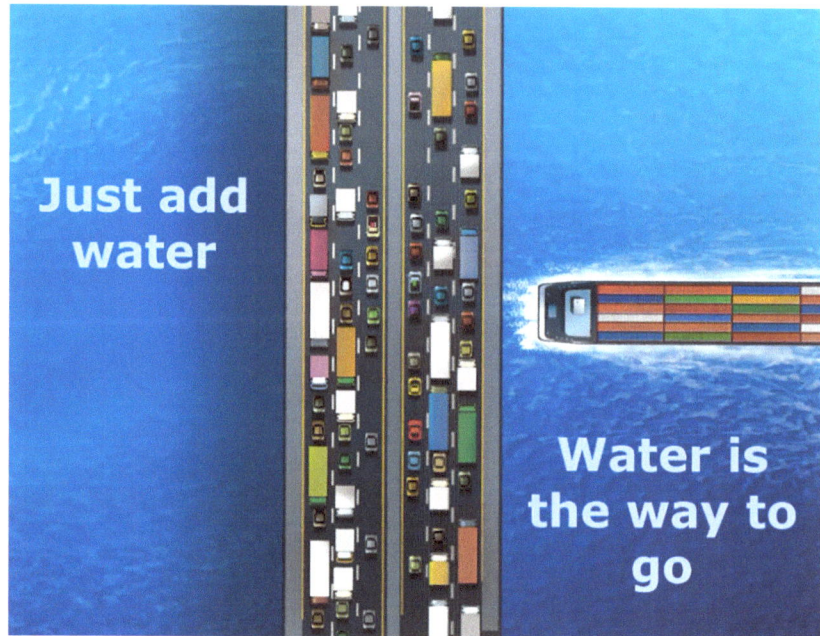

Source: © Inland Navigation Europe. Used with the permission of Inland Navigation Europe. Further permission required for reuse.

part of transport, globally. Most of the world's population resides close to river deltas, coastal areas, and river estuaries. As such, the use of waterways for the transport of all types of goods remains a desirable option. Nonetheless, although many countries are endowed with extensive waterway systems that could support navigation for freight and passengers, currently not many waterways are used for meaningful navigation and transportation of people and freight. Many of the world's rivers (for example, the Amazon, the Nile, the Ganges, and the Volga) that used to anchor national freight and associated economic activities no longer do so. Today, most of those waterways carry insignificant volumes and numbers of people compared with past activity and relative to the size of the economies of the countries in which they are located.

It should be noted that it is difficult to compare inland waterway transportation systems across countries in terms of volumes, fleet size, and navigable waterways because there are no universally accepted definitions of what constitutes an inland waterway transport system. As used in this report, IWT concerns transport on inland waterways (rivers, lakes, and canals). However, in several countries, IWT is defined as domestic transport by water that can include coastal shipping. Meta-analysis of publicly available data reveals important details that help to contextualize IWT globally.

Globalization and global value chains have multiplied the total amount of transported goods worldwide. Therefore, ocean freight has increased, with several types of raw materials, intermediate products, and finished consumer goods crossing continents. Nonetheless, the volume and type of freight transported on most inland waterways has been declining for several decades. With the exception of China, Europe, and the United States, only Vietnam

FIGURE 1.1

Transport volumes of world's busiest inland waterways, 2017

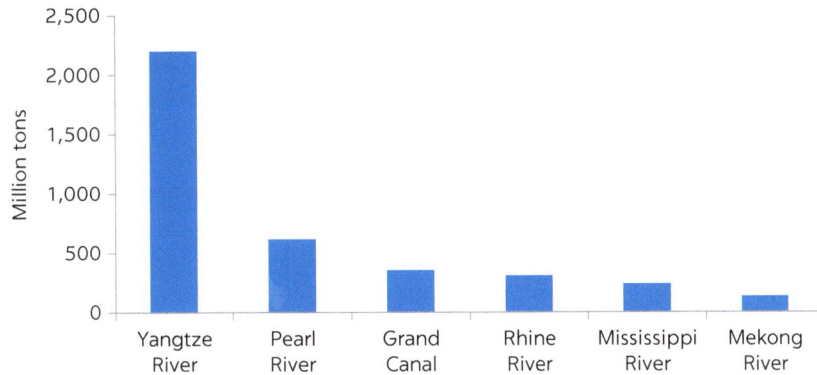

WATERWAY	VOLUME OF TRANSPORTED GOODS (MILLION TONS)
Yangtze River	2,200
Pearl River	662
Grand Canal	354
Rhine River	330
Mississippi River	285
Mekong River	132 (in Vietnam only)

Sources: Data from the China Waterborne Transport Research Institute; CCNR 2018; US Army Corps of Engineers 2017; Vietnam News Agency 2018.

transports more than 200 million tons of cargo a year. In most countries, inland waterways move relatively small quantities of low-value cargo and few passengers. Moreover, the freight and passenger vessels are generally small and outdated. For example, on average, Russia transports 120 million tons, Brazil 55 million tons, Bangladesh 33 million tons, and India 70 million tons (including coastal shipping). Vietnam's fleet of 167,400 vessels carries 17 percent of all cargo in Vietnam, but the average vessel size is below 100 tons; the vast majority of vessels are very small and service mainly local areas. Improving the transport performance in those countries requires modernizing IWT systems and upgrading waterways, facilities, and fleets.

Figure 1.1 shows the volumes of freight carried by the busiest inland waterway systems—each with more than 100 million tons a year. The Yangtze, with 2.2 billion tons of transported goods, is by far the busiest,[1] followed by the Pearl River (622 million tons),[2] the Grand Canal (354 million tons),[3] the Rhine (330 million tons) (CCNR 2018), the Mississippi River (285 million tons),[4] and the Mekong River (132 million tons in Vietnam only).[5]

The looming reality of climate change is shifting the attention of policy makers and leaders across the world toward accelerating the shift to sustainable and smart mobility. Globally, transport accounts for one-quarter of total greenhouse gas (GHG) emissions; however, unlike other sectors such as energy, GHG emissions from transport are still growing. To reduce emissions from transport and meet targets, most countries have committed to promoting IWT as part of their decarbonization agenda. In that respect, multimodal transport needs a strong boost. The European Commission's strategy toward zero emissions by 2050 stipulates that a substantial part of the 75 percent of inland freight carried today by road should shift onto rail and inland waterways. This shift will require measures to better manage and to increase the capacity of railways and inland waterways.

In emerging economies, few policy makers would dispute the economic and environmental arguments for improving IWT in their countries. The comparative advantages of IWT in transporting large quantities over longer distances include safety, sustainability, and cost-efficiency in relation to overall transport costs, energy consumption per ton-kilometer, the low rate of accidents, and low congestion. In China, Europe, and the United States,

IWT has proven to be reliable and environmentally friendly. Emissions from barges per ton-kilometer are lower than those from trains or trucks. A standard 110-meter-long vessel that transports around 3,000 tons of cargo (more than 200 twenty-foot equivalent units, or TEUs) is equivalent to more than 100 journeys taken by a 40-ton truck.

The case is strong for integrating IWT as part of a balanced national or regional transport system. However, most countries struggle to develop the physical infrastructure, institutions, and policies that are needed to revitalize IWT systems that have collapsed. Moreover, changes in global logistics and value chains mean that a dramatic change is needed in the approach to improving IWT and to getting greater private sector involvement for investment, operations, and services. *World Development Report 2020*, published by the World Bank, articulates the importance of global value chains (GVCs) and explains that beginning in the 1990s, changing global logistics and trade patterns enabled unprecedented economic convergence between poor and rich countries. GVCs encompass the cross-country, end-to-end processes by which goods are produced, consumed, and dealt with at the end of their life cycles. Many global and local companies coordinate activities that are needed to produce end products. From luxury products to consumable goods, the label "Made in [country name]" has become less straightforward. It is now widely accepted that the production of any given product will span several suppliers residing across continents. This reality has created opportunities for emerging economies to be part of GVCs and logistics, which in turn contributes to fast economic growth in countries such as China, Mexico, and Vietnam. According to the McKinsey Global Institute, GVCs are experiencing several shifts, including changing global demand (especially toward Asia), growing trade in services, and major technology disruptions. It is estimated that by 2025 emerging markets will consume almost two-thirds of the world's manufactured goods, with products such as cars, building products, and machinery leading the way.

New logistics concepts such as cross-chain control and synchromodality are dramatically changing how goods are moved or processed. These trends are accelerated by disruptive technologies—such as blockchain, big-data analytics, advanced robotics, and artificial intelligence—which are reshaping end-to-end logistics and will inevitably affect the role of carriers and the decisions of shippers. For example, global supply chains increasingly involve multiple participants such as manufacturers, forwarders, shippers, customs agents, and insurers. Innovations in the application of blockchain technology are helping in dispute resolution and improving administrative efficiency and order tracking. Contract logistics companies or various actors in the supply chains can now track all components on an unchangeable and authentic digital ledger. In many cases, the easy coordination of documents on a shared distributed ledger means that physical paperwork is largely unnecessary. Blockchain ensures trustworthy data transfer and sharing across the transportation and logistics ecosystem because the entire network contributes to data validation. The question for policy makers in the countries along the New Silk Road is whether they can adapt fast enough and create the enabling regulatory environment to unleash the potential of these disruptive technologies. The implication for IWT development is that automated and connected multimodal mobility will have an increased role in transportation systems and dramatically affect the infrastructure, vessels, and traffic management systems of the future.

BOX 1.1

Snapshot of China's inland waterways system

China is the world's fourth-largest country, with approximately 9.6 million square kilometers of land. It has 127,000 kilometers of navigable waterways, including 66,200 kilometers that are classified as fairways, of which 12,500 kilometers can accommodate inland vessels of more than 1,000 deadweight tons (DWTs). China also has more than 18,000 kilometers of coastline. China's thousands of mountain ranges, terrains, and plateaus are the source of numerous rivers and lakes. About 1,580 rivers have basin surfaces of more than 1,000 square kilometers. The Yangtze River, with a length of 6,300 kilometers, is the longest and most important river in China. The Yellow River is the second-longest river in China, with a length of 5,464 kilometers.

Because of these dramatic changes in recent decades, countries that are looking to revive their IWT face several uncertainties—and they just have to look to the experiences of Europe and the United States to be informed of them. In addition, the experience of many emerging countries has been a tale of intensive use followed by a total collapse of the IWT sector. China's experience is similar to what many countries are experiencing; its experience offers valuable insights and lessons for other countries not only because of the scale of its revival but also because of the speed of its revival. (Box. 1.1 provides a snapshot of China's inland waterways system.)

EMERGENCE OF INLAND WATERWAY TRANSPORT IN CHINA

China began manufacturing boats about 4,500 years ago. The idea of developing inland waterways dates back to this period of history. Sailing vessels were introduced during the Shang Dynasty (about 1600–1046 BC), when the Yellow River became the main route for transporting agricultural products. To control flooding along the Yellow River and to harness its economic potential, the Chinese tried damming the river by using self-expanding soil. The strategy was innovative for its time, but it failed. Eventually, a strategy was developed to create irrigation channels and to dredge the riverbeds. This method was used to control flooding and to further adapt river flows to foster agricultural development. Those early strategies were the beginnings of developing infrastructure; the following events would build on those early attempts to form the backbone of IWT:[6]

- The first canals were constructed during 770–221 BC, in the Spring and Autumn Period and the Warring States Period. The Hangou Canal was constructed to connect the Yangtze River with the Huaihe River and the Honggou Canal was built to connect the Yellow River with the Huaihe River.
- The Lingqu Canal was constructed during the Qin Dynasty (219–214 BC); it connected tributaries of the Yangtze River and the Pearl River for the first time.
- The Grand Canal (the Jing–Hang Grand Canal), the longest and oldest canal in history, was originally used for military purposes. But connecting China's two major river systems greatly facilitated trade and unlocked the

economic potential of southern China. Its opening, during the Sui Dynasty (AD 581–618), was a milestone in Chinese history. The canal connected five main river systems (the Haihe, the Yellow, the Huaihe, the Yangtze, and the Qiantang). Periodic flooding of the Yellow River posed a danger to the safety and operational use of the Grand Canal, especially during periods of war, when areas were intentionally flooded to keep enemies out. This flooding hindered economic progress and social development.

- During the Sui Dynasty (AD 581–618), the length of the Grand Canal was extended to about 1,700 kilometers. In the tenth century, the pound lock was invented and built. Using miter gates, the Chinese enabled vessels to reach higher elevations.
- During the Yuan Dynasty (1271–1368), the canal was extended to Beijing, which facilitated the transport of grains and other materials from the rich agricultural lands in the south to Beijing. In 2014, UNESCO recognized the Grand Canal as a historic landmark project and registered it as a World Heritage Site.

INLAND WATERWAY TRANSPORT BEFORE THE FOUNDING OF THE PEOPLE'S REPUBLIC OF CHINA

After the Opium War in 1840, international shipping companies entered the Chinese market. Protected by treaties and benefiting from more advanced technologies, international enterprises quickly took control of China's inland shipping market. Chinese-owned shipping enterprises were not able to compete with foreign enterprises.

The first national shipping company in China, the China Merchants Steam Navigation Company (CMSNC), was founded in 1872 to reclaim for China a share of the profits from steam shipping in Chinese waters that had been enjoyed by foreign shipping firms since the early 1860s. It competed mainly with companies from the United States. In 1885, CMSNC became a merchant-managed company under the supervision of the government. CMSNC was the first of several officially supervised and merchant managed industrial enterprises set up by Chinese officials in the late nineteenth century. The company received support from the government that consisted of an exclusive contract to carry the tribute grain (a yearly tax in kind) from the Yangtze Valley to Beijing, as well as loans from government sources and monopoly rights that precluded the founding of rival Chinese steamship companies. By 1909, under the administration of the Ministry of Postal Service and Transmission, the shipping market included 596 shipping companies, with a fleet of 1,092 vessels of various types and a capacity of 147,087 tons. Ten years later, the number of shipping companies and the size of the fleet had more than doubled, and the average vessel size had increased from 135 to 210 deadweight tons (DWTs). In its early history, CMSNC competed successfully with foreign companies, extended routes to Japan and Southeast Asia, and purchased the fleet of the failing American Shanghai Steam Navigation Company. Although it remained one of the four most prominent shipping companies in China between the 1880s and World War II, CMSNC did not grow at the same rate as rival British and Japanese firms.

International shipping companies left the Chinese shipping market temporarily during World War I, which provided an opportunity for CMSNC to grow until after the end of the war. In 1927, CMSNC had a share of only 2.1 percent of total freight volume transported on the Yangtze. After the national government turned it into a fully state-owned enterprise in 1930, its market share rose, growing to 16.4 percent of cargo volume by 1936. The Chinese fleet suffered great losses in the War of Resistance against Japan (1937–45). About 3,000 vessels, with total capacity of 495,320 tons, were destroyed. Despite various initiatives by shipping companies to revive waterway transportation after the victory against Japan, IWT in China did not return to prewar levels for decades.

INLAND WATERWAY TRANSPORT AFTER THE FOUNDING OF THE PEOPLE'S REPUBLIC OF CHINA

The People's Republic of China was officially established on October 1, 1949. Since China's founding, IWT has undergone various stages of development, each with unique characteristics (see table 1.1).

1949–60: Restoration (starting period)

From 1949–60, China's road and rail infrastructures were in serious need of revitalization, but resources were limited. Despite those constraints and relatively small investments, the length of China's navigable waterway network expanded

TABLE 1.1 Key characteristics of China's inland waterway transport's development stages, 1949–present

PERIOD	DESCRIPTION	CHARACTERISTICS
1949–60	Restoration	• More than doubling of size of waterway network • Limited government resources and competing priorities • Huge increase in volumes relative to earlier experiences • Market reform: formation of large, state-owned enterprises
1961–70	Stagnation and decline	• Priority on flood control and agriculture irrigation led to decline • Construction of dams without facilities for IWT • Decrease in size of IWT network • Decrease in IWT volumes
1971–77	International trade driven–development	• Development of heavy industries along Yangtze River • Increase in demand for IWT, especially in low-value bulk • Investments in port infrastructure
1978–90	Gradual recovery	• Social and market reforms: gradual opening up • Restoration of IWT • Infrastructure construction programs • Promotion schemes for IWT
1991–2010	Breakthrough	• Maturing market economy and demand for IWT • Long-term plans for waterways: main axes, ports, terminals • Active promotion and development of IWT
2011–present	Rapid development	• New normal and strong leadership support for IWT • Sustained and reliable policy of accelerating IWT development • Establishment of the Yangtze River Economic Belt • Development of network with trunk lines and tributaries • Focus on quality improvements: environment and safety

Source: Data from the China Waterborne Transport Research Institute.

PHOTO 1.2
Inland waterway transport in the Three Gorges in the 1950s

Source: © Changjiang River Administration of Navigation Affairs, Ministry of Transport. Used with the permission of Changjiang River Administration of Navigation Affairs, Ministry of Transport. Further permission required for reuse.

from 73,600 kilometers in 1949 to 172,000 kilometers in 1960. Freight volumes also increased significantly, rising from 7.63 million tons in 1949 to 294 million tons in 1960.

While infrastructure was being restored, the inland shipping market was reformed. Through public-private partnerships and state funding, new, primarily state-owned inland shipping companies were founded. At the same time, a central planning system was set up for organizing the market. China's largest shipping companies established the Changjiang National Shipping Company (commonly referred to as the CSC Group), to represent state-owned inland shipping companies and to meet transport goals. Photos 1.2 and 1.3 show examples of typical IWT on the Yangtze during the restoration period.

1961–70: Stagnation and decline

During the 1960s, natural disasters and inappropriate strategy hampered national economic development. In response, central government–initiated projects for irrigation, electricity generation, and flood control were needed.

PHOTO 1.3

Traditional shipping on the Yangtze River

Source: © Changjiang River Administration of Navigation Affairs, Ministry of Transport. Used with the permission of Changjiang River Administration of Navigation Affairs, Ministry of Transport. Further permission required for reuse.

IWT was not prioritized, and the inland shipping industry suffered a setback because navigational access to waterways was not considered when dams were constructed. About 1,800 dams in the Yangtze and Pearl River systems did not have any locks, cutting off 19,000 kilometers of waterways and reducing the length of the navigable network to 110,000 kilometers. This decline caused a modal shift from inland waterways to road and rail for large volumes of cargo. In a period of only three years (1961–63), waterborne freight traffic declined by half, to 145 million tons.

Investments in the waterway network were limited and focused on improving three routes:

- The Chuanjiang River and the Jinsha River in the upper reaches of the Yangtze River and the Youjiang River
- The Hongshui River and some tributaries in the upper reaches of the Xijiang River
- Part of the Pearl River system

1971–77: Development driven by international trade

With the restoration of China's status at the United Nations and improvements in relations with the United States, China's economy and international trade experienced rapid growth. Steel, petrochemical, and thermal power industries sprouted along the banks of the Yangtze River, ensuring high demand for transportation of low-value bulk goods on the Yangtze.

The large increase in demand for IWT led to serious capacity constraints at ports and prompted a first wave of port infrastructure expansions. Existing ports were expanded, and several large new terminals, such as the Nanjing crude oil terminal, were built. IWT conditions improved significantly, and shipyards were increasingly busy constructing new vessels. By 1977, total traffic volumes exceeded the previous record volume, which had been achieved in 1960.

PHOTO 1.4
Bulk transport in the 1980s

Source: © Changjiang River Administration of Navigation Affairs, Ministry of Transport. Used with the permission of Changjiang River Administration of Navigation Affairs, Ministry of Transport. Further permission required for reuse.

Photo 1.4 shows a typical vessel that emerged during the period of primary industrial development. The freight turnover of the Yangtze Shipping Bureau reached 30.3 million tons and 15.9 billion ton-kilometers.

1978–90: Gradual recovery

Toward the end of the 1970s, China entered a new period of social and economic reforms, and gradually transformed into a market economy. To build on those reforms, central and local governments responsible for IWT experimented with various programs to stimulate and open the inland shipping market.

Investment and financing systems also changed. Before the 1970s, all ports, waterways, and vessels were publicly financed and organized by the government. This situation gradually changed as the central government's focus narrowed to key areas and support schemes to facilitate the construction of ports and vessels at the provincial level. IWT was gradually restored and new investments were made in infrastructure development. The schemes paid off, with continuously growing freight volumes. Growth averaged 4.3 percent a year during this period, reaching 580 million tons in 1990.

1991–2010: Breakthrough and overall development

China's market economy started to mature in the early 1990s. To prevent infrastructure limitations from holding back economic growth prospects, the Ministry of Transport proposed a long-term plan for the construction of the main highway network and an IWT system comprising major transportation axes, hub ports, terminals, and a traffic support system. The plan for the main IWT routes and ports was derived from various five-year plans and combined into the Eighth Five-Year Plan (1991–95). It gave a huge impetus to the promotion and development of IWT. Photo 1.5 illustrates typical IWT operations in the mid-1990s.

PHOTO 1.5
Inland waterway transport operation in the mid-1990s

Sources: © China Waterborne Transport Research Institute and STC-NESTRA. Used with the permission of China Waterborne Transport Research Institute and STC-NESTRA. Further permission required for reuse.

By the end of 1994, China had about 350,000 inland vessels, with a capacity of more than 20 million tons. Those vessels handled more than 700 million tons of cargo and 900,000 passengers a year, with a turnover of 170 billion ton-kilometers—a huge change relative to 1978. Inland ports handled 870 million tons of cargo, including 15 million tons of international trade cargo and 360,000 TEUs of container transport. In the Yangtze River and the Pearl River Delta regions, IWT became the driving force behind the sustainable growth of transport capacity. Annual transport volume reached 160 million tons in the Jiangsu–Zhejiang section of the Grand Canal and more than 100 million tons on the Pearl River.

At a national conference on IWT in 1995, the Ministry of Transport introduced the plan "one vertical route [the Grand Canal] and three horizontal routes [the Yangtze, Pearl, and Heilongjiang rivers]." The plan initiated a renewed approach of decentralization, including support for infrastructure and fleet development. Under this plan, provinces were given an increased role in developing infrastructure and promoting IWT. During this period, the central

FIGURE 1.2
Length of navigable waterways in China, 1949–2012

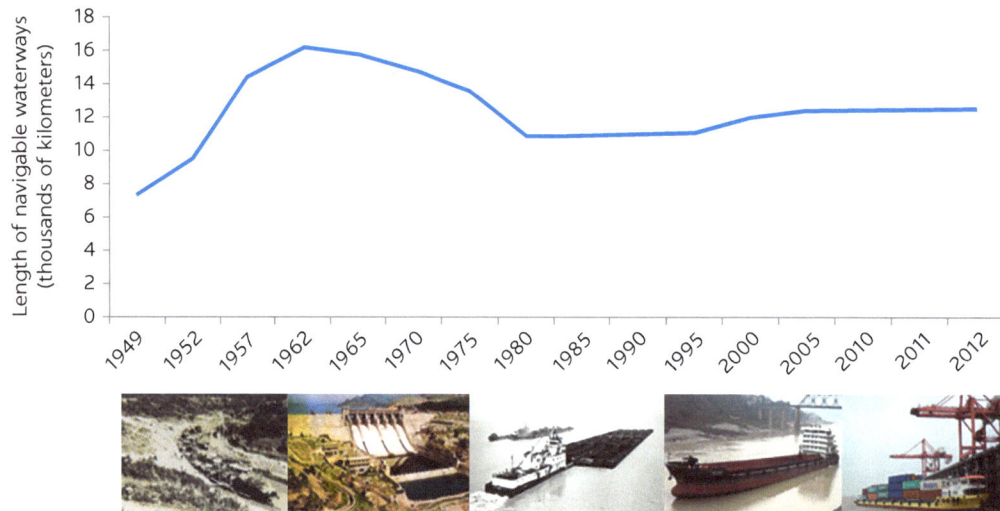

Source: Data from the China Waterborne Transport Research Institute.

government also achieved a landmark with the construction of the Three Gorges Dam (completed in 2006), close to Yichang, and the construction of a ship-lock complex that increased the capacity of the upstream part of the Yangtze River, which allowed larger vessels to operate between Chongqing and Hubei. This capacity increase supported economic development in western China. With the approval of the State Council, an "IWT fund" for the development of inland waterways was established, with a focus on terminal infrastructure construction, such as hubs and main channels. A milestone for IWT in China was the approval of the "Layout Plan of National Inland Waterways and Ports," in 2007. Within the framework of this national plan, IWT development entered an era of systematic management and financing.

2011–Present: Rapid development

In 2000, the Chinese government adopted a "go-west" policy for economic transformation, under which manufacturing industries were gradually relocated to the central and western regions, which lagged the coastal provinces in terms of economic growth. IWT was considered a backbone for the ambitious program of economic transformation. Consequently, in January 2011, the State Council issued a guideline for accelerating development of IWT. It resulted in an upgrading of IWT infrastructure and equipment (photo 1.6). It also recognized the importance of the environmental and cost benefits of IWT for the national agenda and highlighted the importance of IWT. The establishment of the Yangtze River Economic Belt and the Xijiang River Economic Belt confirmed this strategic role for IWT.

In May 2014, the "new normal" was first announced as a major economic policy. It refers to the transition from export-oriented heavy industrial production to increased productivity and domestic consumption. This new policy stance recognized that real GDP growth, which had averaged almost 10 percent a year over the previous three decades, was not sustainable, and that environmental challenges that were a result of rapid economic development over this

PHOTO 1.6
Upgraded infrastructure and equipment in China

Sources: © China Waterborne Transport Research Institute and STC-NESTRA. Used with the permission of China Waterborne Transport Research Institute and STC-NESTRA. Further permission required for reuse.
Note: Clockwise: container cranes, standardized container vessel, roll-on/roll-off transport in Three Gorges, improved terminal layout, entry gate to logistics zone close to container terminal, vessels alongside improved quay wall.

FIGURE 1.3

Investments in inland waterway transport and volumes handled at inland ports in China, 1978–2018

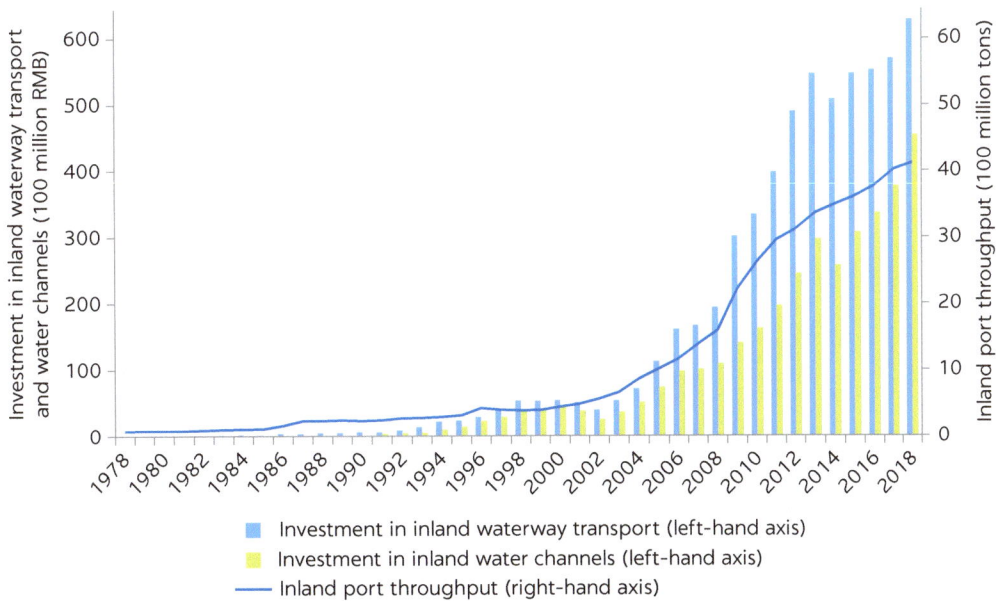

Source: Data from China Waterborne Transport Research Institute.

period adversely affected national aspirations for ecological and environmental protection.

The "new normal" suggests that a comprehensive transport system is needed to facilitate a competitive logistics system for industries and that green and sustainable transport will contribute to a more environment-friendly society. IWT remains a backbone of economic development in the new normal, and as such, it must use land efficiently, be able to transport high volumes at low costs, and have

FIGURE 1.4
GDP and IWT volumes in China, 1978–2018

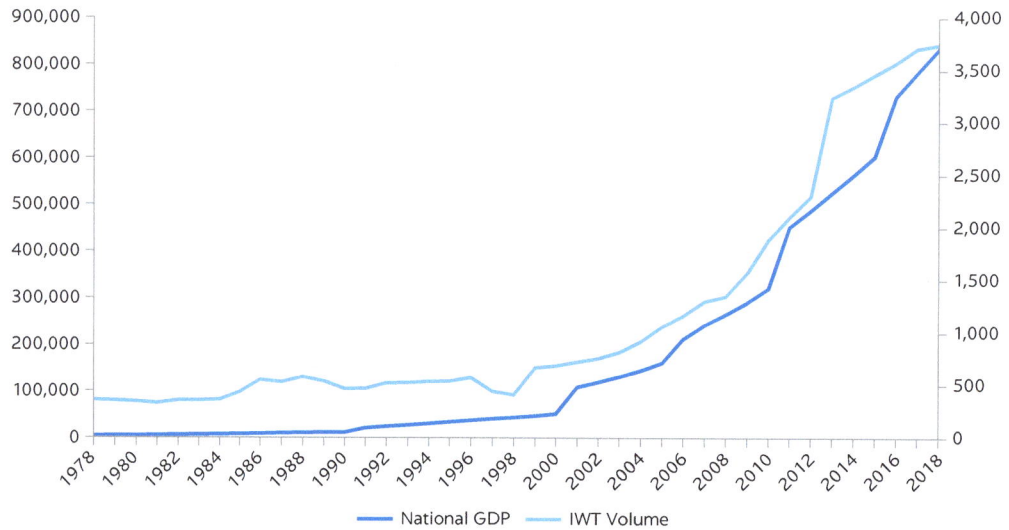

Source: Data from the the China Waterborne Transport Research Institute.

minimal impact on the environment. Because the IWT network can distribute goods across China, it is expected to be one of the top development priorities in Chinese transport strategies in the near future.

In 2016, the Ministry of Transport launched the 13th Five-Year Plan (2016–20). With respect to IWT development, the focus is still on capacity improvements of the Yangtze River, the Xijiang River, the Grand Canal, and other trunk waterways. An important project is the capacity increase of the Yangtze River trunk waterway—what the Chinese call "building the Golden Waterway throughout the river basin"—which will further exploit the economies of scale that IWT has to offer. The new five-year plan includes policies on quality improvements and greening technologies. Investments in IWT and volumes handled at the inland ports soared between 2002 and 2016 (figure 1.3). And over the same period, GDP skyrocketed (figure 1.4).

HIGHLIGHTS

- China's IWT system is the heaviest used in the world, and the Yangtze River is the world's busiest waterway, with 2.3 billion tons transported in 2017.
- Chinese waterways have been of great importance for building the Chinese nation for centuries, but the sector was neglected for a large part of the twentieth century and IWT lost its significance in the transport system because of this neglect.
- China's experience reveals that the revival of inland waterways is possible, not only via investments in infrastructure but also by implementing targeted, sector-specific policies, and sustained high level commitment and actions.

- IWT development has been a critical part of social and economic development in China. IWT was the back bone for China's main economic corridors and continues to be a priority.
- Yangtze River Economic Belt is anchored on IWT on the Yangtze River.
- Recently, environmental imperatives and the need to find solutions to sustainable and smart mobility have placed IWT high on the national agenda.

NOTES

1. Data retrieved from the China Waterborne Transport Research Institute.
2. Data retrieved from the China Waterborne Transport Research Institute.
3. Data retrieved from the China Waterborne Transport Research Institute.
4. Consulted from the American Society of Civil Engineers.
5. Consulted from the Ministry of Transport in Vietnam.
6. An example of such an irrigation system is located on the Minjiang River in Chengdu, in Sichuan Province. The Dujiangyan irrigation system is the oldest grand water conservancy project in the world that is still in use.

REFERENCES

Baichuan Fan. 1985. *Rise of China's Shipping Industry*. Chengdu: Sichuan People's Publishing House.

CCNR (Central Commission for the Navigation of the Rhine). 2018. *Annual Report 2018: Inland Navigation in Europe: Market Observation*. Strasbourg, France. https://www.ccr-zkr.org /files/documents/om/om18_IL_en.pdf#search=%222018%20inland%20navigation%22.

CE Delft. 2017. "Stream Freight Transport 2016: Emissions of Freight Transport Modes, Version 2." CE Delft.

———. 2008. *China's Transportation Opening Up and Reform 30 Years*. Beijing: China Communication Press Co., Ltd.

Dashan, Jia, and Ji Yongbo. 2015. *Strategy of Inland Waterway Transport Advantage*. Beijing: China Communication Press Co., Ltd.

Eurostat. 2017. "Inland Waterway Transport Statistics." Retrieved from *Eurostat Statistics Explained* https://ec.europa.eu/eurostat/statistics-explained/index.php/Inland _waterway_transport_statistics.

Hoang, Dung Anh, Yin Yin Lam, Paul Amos, Paul Reddel, Pham Thi Phuong, Nguyen Thi Phuong Hien. 2019. "Sustainable Development of Inland Waterways Transport in Vietnam: Strengthening the Regulatory, Institutional and Funding Frameworks." World Bank, Washington, DC.

Inland Navigation Europe. 2010. "Just Add Water." Brussels.

US Army Corps of Engineers. 2017. "Waterborne Commerce Statistics for Calendar Year 2017: Waterborne Commerce National Totals and Selected Inland Waterways for Multiple Years." Waterborne Commerce Statistics Center, Institute for Water Resources, US Army Corps of Engineers. https://usace.contentdm.oclc.org/digital/collection/p16021coll2/id/3002/.

US Environmental Protection Agency. 2018. "SmartWay Shipping Partner Tool." Technical Documentation, Washington, DC.

Vietnam News Agency. 2018. "Better Transport Connectivity Needed to Drive Mekong Delta's Development." December 13. https://en.vietnamplus.vn/better-transport-connectivity -needed-to-drive-mekong-deltas-development/143502.vnp.

2 Status of Inland Waterway Transport in China

INTRODUCTION

In 1995, at the first national conference on inland waterway transport (IWT), the Ministry of Transport initiated a plan for building an integrated network of navigable waterways. One of the main goals of the plan was to eliminate bottlenecks in the network. Detailed discussions of the principles of the IWT development master plan and the main waterway channels led to the breakthrough proposal of the 2-1-2 master plan (two horizontal routes, one vertical route, and two networks). At a later stage, the network was expanded by adding tributaries.

In 2007, an important milestone for the development of IWT was achieved with the approval of the "Layout Plan of National Inland Waterway and Ports" by the State Council. This plan laid out the strategic vision for China's IWT network under the umbrella of the "2-1-2-18 network." The plan includes the following components of the national IWT network:

- **Two horizontal routes:** the Yangtze River and the Pearl River trunk waterways
- **One vertical route:** the Grand Canal
- **Two networks:** the Yangtze River Delta and the Pearl River Delta
- **Eighteen high-grade waterways and their tributaries:** 10 tributaries of the Yangtze River basin; three tributaries of the Pearl River basin; and the Huaihe, Shayinghe, Heilongjiang, Songhuajiang, and Min rivers.

Map 2.1 shows the structure of this network. The 2-1-2-18 network articulated a clear and unchanging blueprint and roadmap for the development of IWT in China. Subsequent policy clarifications and investments were targeted at gradually achieving the vision. Unlike many emerging economies that do not have a clear vision for IWT in their countries, China developed a vision for IWT endorsed by the highest level of government, and it was able to align various stakeholders to achieve it within the stated period. This is an important lesson

MAP 2.1
High-grade inland waterways in China, 2018

Source: World Bank map IBRD 45269, August 2020, based on Ministry of Transport.

for emerging economies that are working toward reviving their IWT systems. The 2-1-2-18 network was not a wish list of all IWT from a bygone era that the government set out to achieve; rather, it was the core network needed to support current and projected economic ambitions.

THE CLASSIFIED IWT NETWORK

According to the Ministry of Transport, in 2018 the length of the navigable national inland waterway network was 127,126 kilometers. Of this, 66,200 kilometers (52 percent) are navigable by the smallest commercial vessels (about 50-ton capacity), which can navigate any waterway rated Class VII or higher. Almost 10 percent of the network is classified as Class III or higher. Class III allows for navigation by vessels with 1,000-ton loading capacity. The largest vessels (above 3,000-ton loading capacity) can use only 1 percent of the navigable waterways (table 2.1).

TABLE 2.1 **Length of China's inland waterways, by waterway class, 2018**

WATERWAY CLASS	TYPICAL VESSEL CAPACITY (TONS)	LENGTH (KILOMETERS)	PERCENT OF TOTAL
Substandard		60,684	48
VII	50	17,114	14
VI	100	17,522	14
V	300	7,613	6
IV	500	10,732	8
III	1,000	7,686	6
II	2,000	3,947	3
I	3,000	1,828	1
Total		127,126	100

Source: Data from the China Waterborne Transport Research Institute.

TABLE 2.2 **Length of inland waterway systems in China, by waterway, 2018**

WATERWAY	LENGTH OF NAVIGABLE WATERWAY (KILOMETERS)	PERCENT OF TOTAL
Yangtze River	64,848	51.0
Huai River	17,504	13.8
Pearl River	16,477	13.0
Heilongjiang River	8,211	6.5
Yellow River	3,533	2.8
Min River	1,973	1.6
Grand Canal	1,438	1.1
Other	14,505	11.4
Total	127,126	100

Source: Data from the China Waterborne Transport Research Institute.

The Yangtze River system, including its trunk line and tributaries, has 64,848 kilometers of navigable waterways and accounts for just over half the length of all navigable waterways in China (table 2.2). In relation to the 2-1-2-18 network plan, the Yangtze River basin is also the most heavily used for IWT and underpins a large proportion of the freight activity in China. The Pearl River ranks second in terms of importance on the 2-1-2-18 network plan, but as shown in table 2.2, it has the third-longest navigable waterway. The Grand Canal is only 1,438 kilometers and accounts for just 1 percent of navigable waterways. The Grand Canal is a masterpiece of hydraulic engineering because of its ancient origins and its vast scale, along with its continuous development and its adaptation to circumstances through the ages. Relative to the Yangtze and Pearl, it carries far less freight, but as a designated UNESCO world heritage landmark, it plays an important role in passenger travel and tourism.

Both the United States and the European Union have navigable inland waterways of around 40,000 kilometers. Countries with large navigable waterway systems include Russia (101,670 kilometers), Brazil (63,000 kilometers, of which only 13,000 kilometers is used economically), Vietnam (26,455 kilometers), Bangladesh (24,000 kilometers), and India (20,336 kilometers).

FIGURE 2.1
Handling capacity of berths in China, 2018
DWT

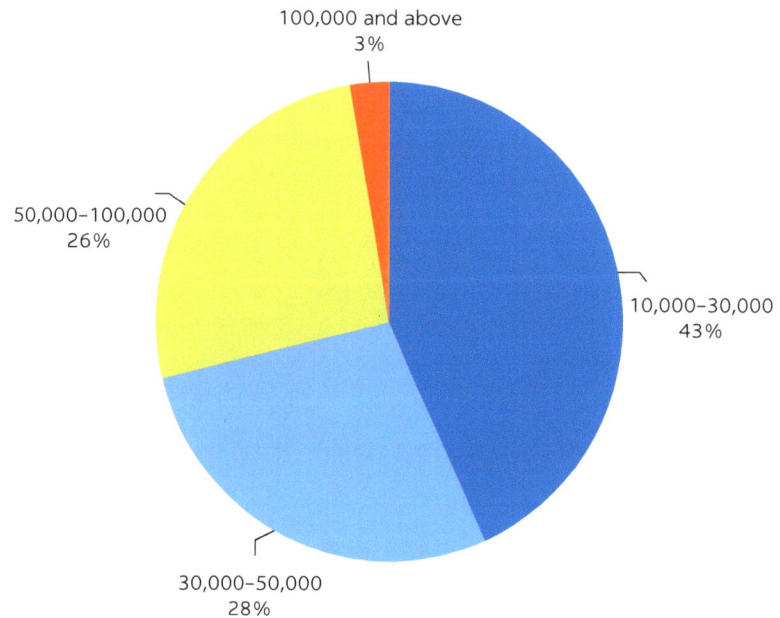

100,000 and above
3%

50,000–100,000
26%

10,000–30,000
43%

30,000–50,000
28%

Source: Data from the China Waterborne Transport Research Institute.
Note: DWT = deadweight ton.

MAIN INLAND PORTS

According to China's Port Law, in 2004, 28 inland ports distributed over the main waterway networks were categorized as major inland ports at the national level. Fifteen of those ports are located in the Yangtze River basin, five are in the Pearl River basin, six are in the Grand Canal and the Huaihe River basin, and two each are in the Heilongjiang River system and the Songliao River basin. (The appendix to this report lists all major ports in the Chinese IWT system.)

The inland port infrastructure has 21,748 inland vessel berths for loading and unloading cargo. Many inland ports (418) are equipped to handle vessels of 10,000 deadweight tons (DWT) and above (figure 2.1). Most of these berths are concentrated in Jiangsu Province and Anhui Province, in the downstream sections of the Yangtze River, which are also accessible to large seagoing and coastal vessels.

INLAND WATERWAY TRANSPORT FLEET

By 2018, China had an active fleet of 124,345 inland vessels with a freight transport capacity of 129.2 million DWT, for an average of about 1,039 DWT per cargo vessel (tables 2.3 and 2.4). Almost 100,000 of these vessels are self-propelled dry bulk vessels. The container fleet numbers 556 vessels, with a total carrying capacity of 338,100 twenty-foot equivalent units (TEUs)—an average of 605 TEUs per vessel.

In addition to cargo vessels, China has 18,682 passenger vessels, about 14 percent of its total fleet. Those passenger vessels have 723,000 seats.

TABLE 2.3 **Composition of China's inland waterway fleet, 2018**

VESSEL TYPE	NUMBER OF VESSELS	PERCENT OF TOTAL
Cargo	93,454	75.2
Passenger	17,651	14.2
Barge	11,148	9.0
Tugboat	1,848	1.5
Tanker	1,495	1.2
Container	556	0.4
Roll-on/roll-off (RoRo)	244	0.2
Total	124,345	100

Source: Data from the China Waterborne Transport Research Institute.

TABLE 2.4 **Capacity of China's inland waterway fleet, 2018**

TYPE OF VESSEL	CAPACITY
Cargo (million DWT)	129.2
Container (1,000 TEU)	338.1
Passenger (1,000 seats)	715.9

Source: Data from the China Waterborne Transport Research Institute.
Note: DWT = deadweight ton; TEU = twenty-foot equivalent unit.

China's inland vessel fleet has by far the largest carrying capacity in the world. The Vietnamese fleet is larger (167,400 vessels), but its average vessel size is below 100 DWT. The European Union has about 20,500 registered inland vessels (about 13,000 self-propelled motor vessels), and the US fleet consists of about 30,000 vessels, most of which are dumb barges. Because of scrapping, upgrading, and standardization programs (described later in the report), the number of vessels has decreased considerably, but the average size has gone up. The net result is an increase in carrying capacity.

FREIGHT VOLUMES CARRIED BY INLAND WATERWAY TRANSPORT

China's inland waterways transport more freight volume than maritime and coastal transport combined. In 2017, about 3,706 million tons of cargo was transported via inland waterways, which is equivalent to almost 1,500 billion ton-kilometers. Table 2.5 shows freight traffic per basin.

TABLE 2.5 **Cargo volumes on China's main river basins, 2017**

WATERWAY	TONS		TON-KILOMETERS	
	MILLIONS	PERCENT OF TOTAL	BILLIONS	PERCENT OF TOTAL
Yangtze River basin	2,209	59.6	1,091.5	73.3
Pearl River basin	622	16.8	129.5	8.7
Grand Canal	354	9.6	104.9	7.0
Heilongjiang River basin	11.9	0.3	0.7	..
Total China	3,706	100	1,488.5	100

Source: Data from the China Waterborne Transport Research Institute.
Note: .. = negligible.

THROUGHPUT AT INLAND PORTS

China's ports handled 14.3 billion tons of throughput in 2018. Inland ports accounted for 34 percent of the output of all Chinese ports, including maritime and coastal ports. Along the Yangtze, cargo throughput was 2.69 billion tons, 55 percent of the total throughput of inland ports. The ports along the Pearl River system handled 951 million tons, 19 percent of the total throughput of inland ports.

Most of the cargo handled at inland ports is domestic. Of the total international trade that is handled at China's ports, about 10 percent (approximately 445 million tons) is handled at inland ports. Container throughput handled by China's major ports was 250 million TEUs in 2018, of which inland ports handled 28.6 million TEUs (11 percent). The container segment of the market is still increasing by double digits (rising by 6 percent from 2017 to 2018).

Table 2.6 and map 2.2 show the 10 inland ports with the highest cargo throughput in 2018.

MAP 2.2

Location of China's top 10 inland ports, 2018

Source: World Bank map IBRD 45270, August 2020, based on China Waterborne Transport Research Institute.

TABLE 2.6 **Top 10 inland ports in China, by cargo throughput, 2018**

RANK	PORT	THROUGHPUT (MILLION TONS)	SHARE OF TOTAL INLAND PORTS (PERCENT)
1	Suzhou	532	12.9
2	Nantong	267	6.5
3	Nanjing	252	6.1
4	Taizhou	245	5.9
5	Chongqing	204	5.0
6	Jiangyin	176	4.3
7	Zhanjiang	153	3.7
8	Wuhu	120	2.9
9	Hangzhou	118	2.9
10	Jiujiang	117	2.8
	Total top 10	2,185	53

Source: Data from the China Waterborne Transport Research Institute.

PASSENGER VOLUMES ON INLAND WATERWAYS

Passenger traffic in China decreased between 1987 and 2003, partly because of the building of many bridges, which obviated the need for ferries. The decline was particularly steep between 1987 and 2004, when the development of railway lines parallel to the Yangtze reduced passenger services along the waterways. After 2004, passenger traffic increased again, thanks in part to the growing river cruise sector, marking the change from regular passenger services to recreational use and tourism. In 2018, the number of passenger trips was approximately 280 million (figure 2.2). The trend of increasing passenger transit for recreational purposes is not unique to China.

FIGURE 2.2

Passenger traffic on China's waterways, 1978–2018

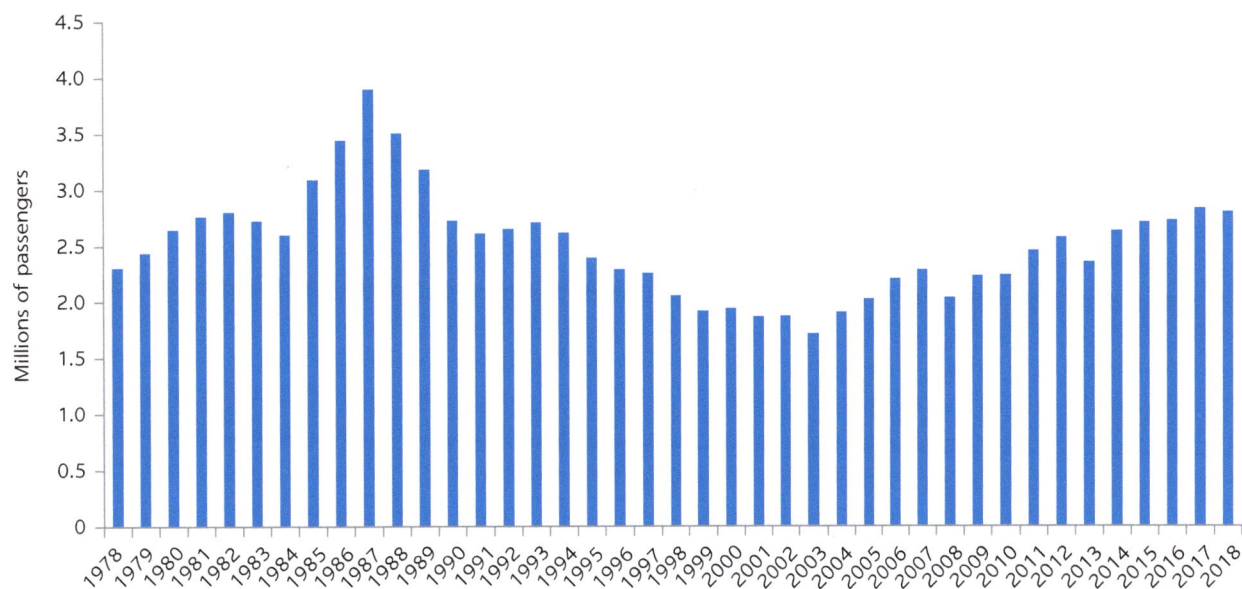

Source: Data from the China Waterborne Transport Research Institute.

PHOTO 2.1
Modern passenger transport facilities in China

Source: © Changjiang River Administration of Navigation Affairs, Ministry of Transport. Used with the permission of Changjiang River Administration of Navigation Affairs, Ministry of Transport. Further permission required for reuse.

Beginning in 2010, other river basins—such as the Rhine/Danube, Nile, Mississippi, Mekong, and Ganges—have experienced dramatic increases in luxury river cruises.

China's main ports handled 177 million passengers in 2018, a little more than half of which (89 million) came through inland ports. The most important inland ports for passenger traffic are Chongqing (6.86 million passengers), Yichang (1.8 million passengers), Foshan (570,000), and Guang'an (520,000). Chongqing and Yichang are important for river cruises through the Three Gorges basin. Photo 2.1 shows a modern passenger terminal on the Yangtze River and several cruise and tourist vessels.

HIGHLIGHTS

The following characteristics of China's IWT development were key:

- The development of a well-analyzed long-term plan that provides a clear and consistent framework for action. The State Council approved the "Layout Plan of National Inland Waterways and Ports." This document outlined the strategic vision for China's IWT network under the umbrella of the "2-1-2-18 network."
- The 2-1-2-18 network was simple and easily understood by all stakeholders. Importantly, it was not a wish list of all IWT from a bygone era that the government set out to achieve; rather, it was the core network needed to support current and projected economic ambitions.
- The 2-1-2-18 strategic IWT network plan received strong government endorsement and consistent high-level support for implementation, including sustained policy clarifications and financing.
- Five-year development plans detailed the implementation of the 2-1-2-18 strategy, setting out the work program for each plan period; once decided, these plans are rarely changed, providing a clear framework within which local governments and the construction/supply industry can plan with confidence.
- Minimal changes to individual project plans once they are approved.

- Classification of the waterways was an important first step; following that step, the development of the river fleet and the ports could then be synchronized.
- Passenger transport changed from regular transport for river crossing and longitudinal public transport to tourism and cruising.

REFERENCE

Ministry of Transport, China. 2007. "Layout Plan of National Inland Waterways and Ports," National Development and Reform Committee, Beijing.

3 Reforming and Developing Inland Waterway Transport in China

FORTY YEARS OF SUSTAINED IWT REFORM IN CHINA

For many years, China's inland waterway transport (IWT) system received little support from the government, and it was not considered a major mode of transport. IWT was considered a dirty and outdated mode of transport for both goods and passengers. This thinking has changed in the past 40 years. Now, IWT is viewed as an important component of a more sustainable transport system that is an integral part of national priorities for sustainable economic and social development, and a pillar for environmental sustainability.

The previous chapter provided facts and figures of the IWT system in China. This chapter describes how the IWT system was achieved, and it covers the reforms that transformed China's IWT system from an outdated, slow mode of transport for bulky low-value goods to a highly competitive system carrying all kinds of cargo, including high-value containerized goods.

Table 3.1 summarizes the main sector reforms during the 40-year period of rapid IWT development.

NATIONAL WATERWAY PLANNING AND HIGH-LEVEL SUPPORT FOR IWT DEVELOPMENT

The development of IWT is closely related to the development of the economy and trade. Because IWT was clearly identified as being closely linked to the core economic corridors, it has been influenced by major strategic decisions in China.

Prior to 1970, IWT received little attention from policy makers. The role of waterways was limited to agriculture, irrigation, and hydropower. The year 1971 was a landmark for China, and it triggered a renewed policy focus on the development of IWT in China. On October 25, 1971, the United Nations General Assembly Resolution 2758 recognized the "People's Republic of China" as "the only legitimate representative of China to the United Nations"; Sino-US relations improved, and China's economy and foreign trade developed rapidly. Large enterprises established along the Yangtze River (typically manufacturers of steel products, petrochemical products, and thermal power) laid the foundation for

TABLE 3.1 Efforts by the Chinese government to improve inland waterway transport, 1978–present

PERIOD	FOCUS	ACTIVITIES
1978–90	• Extension of the navigable channel network: most ad hoc and reactive to tackle major infrastructure bottlenecks	• Implementation of critical infrastructure projects: • North section of the Grand Canal in Jiangsu Province • Phase 1 of the Xi River project • Phase 1 of the Xiang River project • Construction of the Gezhouba Dam and Lock project on the Yangtze • Canalization of more than 1,500 kilometers of channels • Establishment of joint coordination and working group on dams without navigation facilities • State Council approval of Yangtze Shipping Institutional Reform Plan to open up the IWT market and improve capacity
1991–2000	• Financial reforms and experimentation; attracting alternative financing • Development of standards and revision specifications • Construction of major infrastructure	• Convening of national IWT conference and establishment of special IWT fund • Development and approval of IWT standards • Issuance of regulations by the Ministry of Transport on levying and using IWT maintenance fee • Promotion of use of loans from international institutions, including the World Bank • Beginning of the Three Gorges Dam and Locks project
2001–11	Improvement of river-sea connectivity	• Development of the Yangtze Golden Waterway • Improvement of the Yangtze Delta high-grade waterway network • Implementation of the barge standardization program • Establishment of a leading coordination group for strengthening transport on Yangtze River • Issuance of the implementation plan for the Yangtze Golden Waterway construction under the 11th Five-Year Plan (2006–10)
2012–today	• Sustainable development of IWT to strengthen its role in a comprehensive transport system	• Issuance by the State Council of guidelines on strengthening the Yangtze and IWT development and guidelines on promoting Yangtze River Economic Belt development by promoting Golden Waterway development • Issuance of a master plan on comprehensive transport corridors of the Yangtze River Economic Belt • Issuance of Ministry of Transport's guidelines on promoting green development in the Yangtze River Economic Belt • Adoption of an implementation plan focused on intermodal development along the Yangtze River Economic Belt • Issuance of a three-year action program to promote intermodal development • Extension of a 12.5-meter deep channel in the downstream section of the Yangtze to Nanjing

Source: Data from the China Waterborne Transport Research Institute.

the development of bulk cargo transportation along the river. Soaring demand led to the severe congestion of Chinese ports. By 1977, several 10,000-ton terminals had been built, and port capacity had expanded throughout the country.

After the Third Plenary Session of the 11th Central Committee of the Communist Party of China in 1978, China adopted a policy to open up the economy. Subsequently, the economic system gradually shifted from a single planned economy to a more market-oriented economy.

The rapid development of China's economy and foreign trade continued, further increasing demand for IWT. Capacity constraints in the shipping and port sectors resulted in major delays of ships and goods. To stimulate the IWT market, the Ministry of Transport prepared detailed policies and institutional reforms aimed at accelerating the development of the sector. For example, to meet the demands of accelerating development, in 1982 the Ministry of Transport announced the formation of a new IWT administration. The Ministry of Transport also implemented various infrastructure projects. It extended the northern Jiangsu section of the Grand Canal, launched phase 1 of the Xijiang

River navigation construction project and the Xiangjiang River regulation project, and began the Hanjiang River navigation construction project. In addition, more than 1,500 waterways were canalized. A number of large-scale navigation lock projects were initiated to reestablish accessibility to navigable waterways that had been closed off. One major project was the Gezhouba Dam (photo 3.1) on the Yangtze—now located 38 kilometers downstream of the Three Gorges Dam—which was coordinated jointly by the Ministry of Transport and the Ministry of Water Resources.

New concepts entered the market. Push convoys—consisting of push boats/tugs and barges—increased the scale of IWT operations. Container transport was introduced after the State Development Planning Commission recognized multimodal transport solutions and following pilot projects for river container transport that were initiated by the Ministry of Transport in 1989.

In the 1990s, China accelerated reforms and further opened up the national economy to foreign trade, which developed rapidly. Between 1990 and 1995, gross domestic product grew at an average annual rate of 10.4 percent, and the growth of foreign trade averaged 15.2 percent. Production was further industrialized, increasing the demand for IWT and higher levels of service. Between 1990 and 1995, the average annual growth rate of throughput at inland ports was 5.9 percent, with throughput reaching 925 million tons by 1995; transported volumes rose by 7.6 percent a year, reaching 831 million tons in 1995. Volumes transported along the Yangtze River rose rapidly during this period. The Sunan Canal, near Suzhou, was constructed and quickly attracted significant cargo volumes.

The critical role of IWT development and the effect policy reforms were having on overall economic development were obvious to policy makers in central government, provincial governments, industry, and decision makers. The link between reforms and investments on the one hand and outstanding economic outcomes on the other hand was unmistakable. However, major challenges faced the sector, making an urgent response from IWT even more important if targeted economic growth was going to be achieved. To address these challenges, the Ministry of Transport organized a conference in 1995, the first national conference in Chinese history to focus exclusively on addressing the challenges in the IWT sector. Two of the main goals were to eliminate bottlenecks in the network and to improve the capabilities of shipping companies and waterway management agencies. Experts were invited to submit opinions from

PHOTO 3.1

Gezhouba dam and ship lock in Yichang

Sources: © China Waterborne Transport Research Institute and STC-NESTRA. Used with the permission of China Waterborne Transport Research Institute and STC-NESTRA. Further permission required for reuse.
Note: The left picture is from the early 1980s; the right picture is from the mid-1990s.

across the spectrum of academia, industry, and the public sector. The Ministry of Transport announced that further stimulation of IWT should be a joint effort of central and provincial-level governments. The redistribution of responsibilities across governmental levels was key to building an integrated waterway network of waterways, ports, wharfs, supporting safety systems, and new transport services. This redistribution was a major shift in the way IWT was developed because prior to this date most functions were centralized.

The 1995 conference was a milestone in the history of China's IWT development. During the conference, a consensus about the significance of IWT for the economy was forged. The principles of the IWT development master plan and the main waterway channels were discussed in detail, which led to the proposal of the 2-1-2 master plan and related priorities to develop the sector. The principle of "overall planning at the center with layered responsibilities, and joint construction" of IWT was confirmed. Central, local, and all other resources were crowded to finance IWT development. The policy of diversified investments was set up as a main resource, combined with multichannel financing instruments. During the conference, it was also decided to put more effort into researching key technologies to address navigational challenges of the Three Gorges Dam project and standardization of barges. That year, the State Council approved the establishment of an IWT fund that would finance the construction of new waterways and port infrastructure and regulate waterways. Rapid construction of major infrastructure was a key outcome of this reform. More than 29,000 berths—including 133 berths of 10,000 tons—were commissioned, thereby relieving bottlenecks and constraints in handling capacity.

The 11th Five-Year Plan for National Economic and Social Development of China (2006–10) was another turning point for IWT in China. At a strategic level, the plan set out to achieve more balanced development between urban and rural areas. Crucially, it included a high-level push for "improving the inland waterways navigation conditions, stimulating the Yangtze River Golden Waterway and the high-grade waterway networks in the Yangtze River Delta and the Pearl River Delta." Under the plan, the IWT sector was included in the list of strategic industries for social and economic development. Subsequent policies clarified various dimensions, such as promotion of an energy-efficient, integrated transport system and accelerating the development of IWT. To implement the strategic requirements of the Chinese leadership, in November 2005 a high-level forum on the "rational construction of a Golden Waterway to promote economic development of the Yangtze River" was held. The Ministry of Transport and the provincial governments along the Yangtze River participated in the forum. Participants endorsed a plan for promoting the construction of the Yangtze River Golden Waterway during the 11th Five-Year Plan, marking a new beginning for the construction of IWT, with a focus on the Yangtze River Golden Waterway. The plan played an important role in guiding and promoting the development of water transport along the Yangtze River and IWT in other parts of China. Following this plan, each province issued a scheme for implementation. For example, since 2007, the Department of Finance of Jiangsu Province has allocated dedicated funds of more than ¥500 million per year to improve inland waterways such as the Yangtze River and to establish a joint conference system for accelerating the development of water transport. The construction of the Yangtze River Golden Waterway has been listed as an important responsibility of governments of all levels along the river. The Hubei provincial government has devoted ¥100 million per year to facilitate the development of IWT.

In 2007, China and the Netherlands held the Yangtze Summit in Wuhan. The ministers of transport of the two countries delivered keynote speeches at this important summit, at which knowledge and ideas were exchanged on policy, planning, port development, barge standardization, transportation safety, and information and communication technology (ICT). They articulated specific areas that gave new impetus to initiatives to further promote the development and use of IWT.

In 2011, the State Council issued the "Guideline of the State Council on Speeding Up the Development of Inland Waterway Transport Including the Yangtze River," which indicated that the development of IWT had become a national strategic priority. The guideline provided a new opportunity for strategic developments along the Yangtze River Economic Belt and the Xijiang River Economic Belt, among other areas, specifically citing the role of IWT. This 2011 guideline was followed by the State Council's 2014 "Guideline on Promoting the Development of the Yangtze River Economic Belt by Relying on the Golden Waterway," which cited the need to give full play to the advantages of the Yangtze River, such as the capacity, low cost, and low energy consumption of IWT; to accelerate the improvement of the trunk waterway system of the Yangtze River; to regulate and dredge the downstream waterways; to effectively ease the bottlenecks of the upper and middle reaches; to improve the navigation conditions of tributaries; to optimize the functional layout of ports; to strengthen the construction of a collecting and dispatching system; to develop combined river-sea transportation and direct transport between trunk and branch waterways; and to create a smooth, efficient, safe, and green golden waterway.

On January 4, 2016, the president of China made an inspection visit to Chongqing, where he stressed that in promoting the development of the Yangtze River Economic Belt, long-term national interests must be considered in line with the mitigation of adverse environmental and ecological effects. He emphasized that the restoration of the ecological environment of the Yangtze River should be a priority and that stakeholders should work together to ensure environmental protection and stop large-scale development. This marked an important divergence from a focus mostly on economic and social goals to consideration of environmental concerns. To follow up, on August 4, 2017, the Ministry of Transport formulated and issued the "Guideline on Promoting the Green Shipping Development of the Yangtze River Economic Belt." This guideline detailed how to implement IWT development that paid equal importance to social, economic, and environmental concerns. As part of the 13th Five-year Plan (2016–20), specific details about how to promote multimodal transport along the Yangtze River Economic Belt were outlined.

It is clear that IWT in China has developed rapidly because of the sustained support for the sector at the highest level backed by the clear emphasis of the role that IWT plays in social, economic, and environmental national priorities of China. IWT is directly linked to prosperity and the future of China. Between 1973 (when the requirement for "changing the situation of ports in three years" was put forward) and 2011, six Chinese prime ministers or vice prime ministers have delivered 11 high-level speeches about the importance of developing IWT. The State Council, the National Development and Reform Commission, and other national institutions issued requirements for developing IWT and provided support for institutional mechanisms, funds, and policies. This support has been key to the fundamental change and rapid development of China's IWT during 40 years of reform.

Reforms and rapid growth were guided by the five-year plans, which provided detailed plans and funded priorities for step-by-step development of IWT in China. Crucially, those plans were not wish lists and generally they remained unchanged, making it possible to achieve sustained development during the 40 years of reform. Table 3.2 summarizes the key elements of the five-year plans from 2001 onward.

In general, it is evident from the IWT sector in China that economic policies and IWT development strategy go hand in hand. Development of large-scale industrial activity along the Yangtze River called for a high-capacity, low-cost transport system: IWT. The go-west policy would not have been as successful as it was (figure 3.1) without upgrading the middle and upper parts of the Yangtze River and investing heavily in IWT infrastructure and transshipment facilities along the river.

TABLE 3.2 Development of inland waterway transport under China's 10th–13th five-year plans

FIVE-YEAR PLAN	MAIN GOALS
10th (2001–05)	• Further develop and increase the capacity of the main waterways under the 2-1-2 network[a] (which includes the Yangtze River trunk line, the Pearl River trunk line, the Grand Canal, the Yangtze River Delta, and the Pearl River Delta) by bringing the navigational channels to similar classification levels. • Strengthen the capacities of the main inland ports. • Optimize the structure of inland ports and fleet, container, bulk, and RoRo transport. • Strengthen coordination and develop navigational facilities for dams without navigation function.
11th (2006–10)	• Further develop and increase the capacity of the main waterways under the 2-1-2-18 strategic IWT network.[b] • Develop a container feeder inland transport network to the Port of Shanghai at the Yangtze Delta to improve intermodal connections. • Strengthen the navigational capacity of the main side/tributary rivers through canalization projects, including electric navigation complexes. • Strengthen the container terminal capabilities of main inland ports and improve logistics services (by improving custom services, for example). • Prioritize sea-river, container, and RoRo vessels and encourage the development of inland cruise vessels to further standardize the fleet. • Strengthen safety and emergency and response facilities by developing dynamic traffic management and information technology (IT) systems.
12th (2011–15)	• Further develop and increase the capacity of main waterways so that 70 percent of the 2-1-2-18 network reaches the targeted navigation grades. • Strengthen rail and highway connections at main inland ports and improve logistics services to better promote industrial development near main inland ports. • Prioritize sea-river, container, and RoRo vessels to further standardize the fleet. • Develop a comprehensive IWT information service system. • Promote green development of inland ports and transport from the perspectives of management, technology application, and transport optimization.
13th (2016–20)	• Further develop and increase the capacity of main waterways so that 90 percent of the 2-1-2-18 network reaches the targeted navigation grades. To increase the capacity of the Three Gorges Dam navigational facilities by all means, including a better IT system, strengthen the bypassing road and rail transport system. • Further strengthen the rail and highway connections of main inland ports and expand some inland ports (such as the hub function of Chongqing and Wuhan), and continue to improve logistics services to promote local economic development. • Further standardize the fleet so that 70 percent of the inland fleet is standardized by 2020 and promote the development of specialized vessels. • Strengthen the coordination, collaboration, and integration of river information systems along the Yangtze, develop a digital Yangtze trunk-line waterway system, and strengthen the dynamic Yangtze safety management system. • Promote green developments and build up an eco-IWT system through the application of stricter shoreline management and green technologies at inland ports and promote the use of vessels by liquified natural gas.

Note: RoRo = roll-on/roll-off.

a. The 2-1-2 network refers to two horizontal routes (the Yangtze trunk waterway and the Pearl River trunk waterway), one vertical route (the Grand Canal), and two networks (the Yangtze River Delta and the Pearl River Delta).

b. The 2-1-2-18 network adds to the 2-1-2 network 18 high-grade waterways and their tributaries (10 tributaries of the Yangtze River basin; three tributaries of the Pearl River basin; and the Huaihe, Shayinghe, Heilongjiang, Songhuajiang and Min rivers).

Although waterway transportation has had a long history in Europe, recently the importance of IWT has increased even more as policy makers seek to shift freight to more environmentally friendly modes. In response to the Paris Agreement, many governments, associations, and businesses are setting bold climate targets. The ambition is for Europe to be the first climate-neutral continent in the world by 2050. A policy framework and development program are in place to stimulate and promote the use of IWT in Europe (box 3.1).

FIGURE 3.1

Value of industrial output in provinces along the Yangtze River, 2017

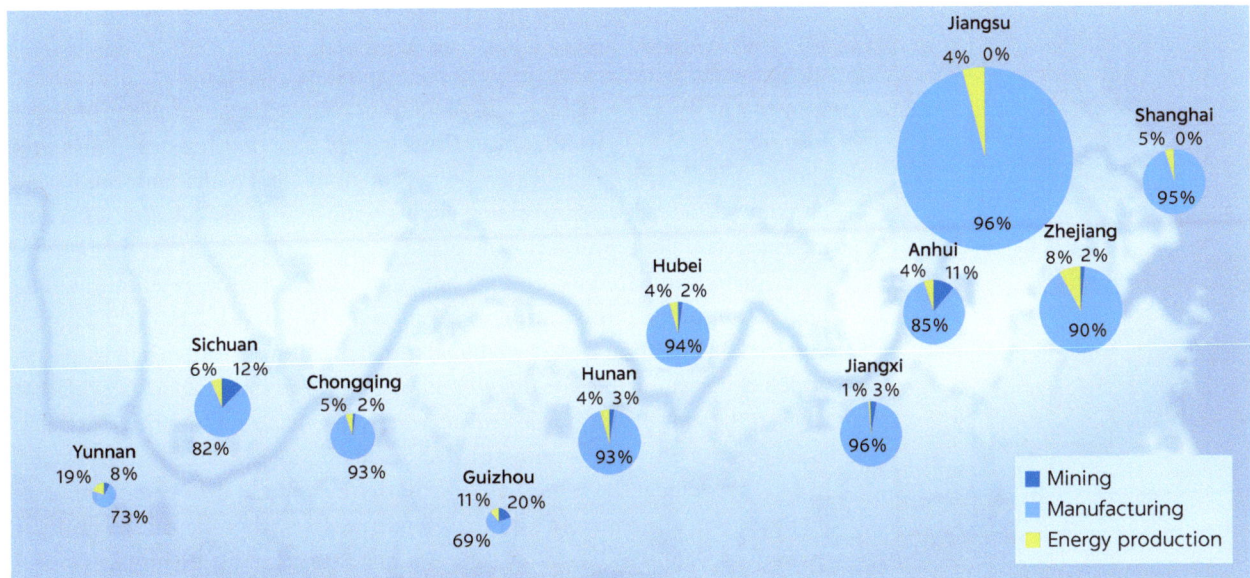

Source: Based on data from China Waterborne Transport Research Institute.

BOX 3.1

Support for inland waterways in Europe

The European Union is focusing on how IWT can make a greater contribution to the European economy and to offsetting the costs of transport to society, such as pollution, traffic accidents, and road congestion. Given that IWT has the capacity to accommodate much more traffic than it currently does, only limited investment in transport infrastructure is needed to meet those goals.

In 2006, the European Commission adopted a communication on the promotion of IWT. The Navigation and Inland Waterway Action and Development in Europe (NAIADES) Action Program, intended for 2006–13, focused on five strategic areas for a comprehensive IWT policy: market, fleet, jobs and skills, image, and infrastructure. Those measures are rounded off by reflections on an improved organizational structure. Issues addressed under

NAIADES I include working time arrangements, professional qualification requirements, administrative and regulatory barriers, innovative technologies (such as river information services), and infrastructure improvements. By creating favorable conditions for the further development of the sector, the European Commission aimed to encourage more companies to use IWT. From the program, the European Commission concluded that the IWT sector needed additional specific support, given the entry barriers to the market and the high initial cost of setting up a new service. The NAIADES program was extended. The NAIADES II package, "Towards Quality Inland Waterway Transport," aims to create the conditions that can make inland navigation a high-quality mode of transport. It sets out the European Union's program for policy action in the field of IWT for 2014–20.

INSTITUTIONAL REFORM AND ADMINISTRATION OF INLAND WATERWAY TRANSPORT IN CHINA

Governance framework of inland waterway transport in China

China's management model for waterways transport is complex, with responsibilities spread over many institutions at the national, regional, and provincial levels. This complex institutional framework has evolved over time and has served to address specific challenges during the period of rapid economic development. As stipulated in China's Water Law, the Ministry of Water Resources is the supreme administrative department responsible for the overall management and coordination of water resources. Specialized plans for IWT infrastructure and ports must be coordinated through the Ministry of Water Resources, which then coordinates the overall use of water resources. Also, it is stipulated in China's Port Law that the design of ports should accord with national, provincial, and municipal plans, and should also be compatible with other plans, such as those for land use, cities, river management, flood prevention, oceanic regions, other transport modes, and other plans stipulated in relevant laws and administrative regulations. The Regulation on Administration of Waterways stipulates that the activities undertaken by national and provincial transport administrative departments, which are responsible for development plans and engineering designs of river and canal projects relevant to water resources and hydroelectricity, must consult with the administrative departments of water resources and hydroelectricity at the same level, and with forestry and fishery departments if appropriate. Conversely, all other departments with policies and projects that affect water resources also should take into account the impact on and needs of IWT. Within this overarching framework, the central Ministry of Transport (MoT) has the overall responsibility for policy and administration of IWT in China. As stipulated in the Regulation on Administration of Waterways, MoT is responsible for planning waterways of national importance, which include the Class IV and higher channels (suitable for vessels of 500 tons-plus) that are part of the national network, plus the Class V and better waterways (suitable for vessels of 300 tons-plus) that have important transprovincial traffic functions.

MoT has decentralized responsibility for the day-to-day administration and management of the main waterways of national importance to the Yangtze River Authority and the Pearl River Authority, which are agencies of MoT. Provincial governments are responsible for most other waterways, and for most of the total network, which they administer through provincial navigation authorities. Both the two main MoT navigation authorities, and the provincial navigation authorities, have a similar schedule of responsibilities, although those responsibilities apply to the waterways under their own jurisdictions.

The technical regulations for vessels and crews are set nationally by MoT, but vessel surveys and registration are undertaken by the provincial navigation authorities. It is believed that there is a significant divergence between provinces in their compliance with the national standards, partly because of an attempt by some provinces to encourage vessels to register in their jurisdiction and partly because of a concern by some provinces that poorer operators cannot afford to meet the standards and might be forced out of business. Each provincial navigation authority drafts a plan for the waterways under its supervision, consistent with national waterway planning policies. The plan is implemented after approval by provincial governments and is submitted as a record to MoT at the same time. If the channel crosses between provinces, the plan must be agreed on by all of the relevant provinces.

Management and administration of IWT in China

There is no blueprint for inland waterway management and operations that can be directly replicated and easily applied elsewhere. The systems in place in the world's main waterway countries reflect their histories, international setting, and government policies on efficiency and transparency in public service and the role and involvement of the private sector.

In China, several bodies are responsible for IWT at the national level and many are responsible at the local level. At the national level are the State Council, the National Development and Reform Commission (NDRC), and the Ministry of Transport; the main player at the local level is the provincial government.

- The State Council is responsible for formulating the overall national policy and approving the implementation of industrial policy. All ministries and commissions are constituent units of the State Council.
- The NDRC is a macroeconomic regulation and control department that studies and formulates economic and social development policies and carries out and directs reform of the overall economic system. It is also responsible for (a) formulating and organizing the implementation of national economic and social development strategies, as well as medium- and long-term plans and annual plans; (b) promoting and coordinating the comprehensive reform of the economic system; and (c) participating in the formulation of industrial policies, the promotion of sustainable development, and the formulation and implementation of price policies.
- The Ministry of Transport is responsible for promoting the construction of the national comprehensive transportation system; crafting overall plans for the development of railway, highway, waterway, civil aviation, and postal industries; formulating waterway development strategies, plans, and policies; and establishing standards to link modes of transport. It needs State Council approval for major inland waterway transport policies. In some cases, the State Council will entrust the NDRC to participate in policy formulation and implementation.
- Provincial governments carry out administrative work in their provinces. For the implementation of IWT policies, the Ministry of Transport usually works in conjunction with the port and navigation management departments of the provincial transport offices.

In addition to those institutions, the Ministry of Water Resources (MWR) plays an important role. It is responsible for the unified management and supervision of water resources throughout the country. Its seven river basin management committees manage the use of water resources within their basins. The needs of urban and rural residents should be satisfied first when developing and using water resources. The needs of agriculture, industry, the environment, and shipping should also be considered. Ecological needs should be fully considered, especially in arid and semi-arid areas. When constructing and operating a ship lock, the water conservancy department and the transportation department must communicate with each other. The inland ship lock usually takes account of flood control, irrigation, and power generation. The water conservancy department also needs to coordinate transportation and water conservancy personnel to use and dispatch water resources.

Many countries are discovering (or rediscovering) the value of a good IWT system and reinvesting in IWT, with the aim of better integrating it into the transportation matrix. International bodies and financial institutions—such as the European Commission, the World Bank, the Asian Development Bank, and the United Nations Economic Commission for Europe—are increasingly committed to and engaged in the development of IWT.

Examples from Europe and the United States offer different models. China's model has characteristics of both the United States' and Europe's models, but it also exhibits unique characteristics.

The management of IWT in the United States, in principle, has several similarities to China. In both China and the United States, the IWT systems are predominantly sovereign national waterways. Moreover, both countries are federal in nature with strong subsovereign divisions of government. In China, these subsovereign divisions are the provinces, and in the United States, they are the states. Nevertheless, despite these similarities, the approaches that the United States and China have adopted for sector governance are quite different. Box 3.2 describes IWT management in the United States.

In the United States, the federal government (through the US Department of Transportation's Maritime Administration) is responsible for overall IWT policy. But the management and operation of the IWT network is almost wholly delivered by a single, integrated military agency—the US Army Corps of Engineers. The states themselves have no executive role in IWT policy or the administration of navigation infrastructure, except through consultative mechanisms and contributing to the funding of projects, which they might sponsor. Different from China, IWT in the United States falls under the US Department

BOX 3.2

Managing IWT in the United States

Two federal government agencies are responsible for the IWT system in the United States: the Maritime Administration (MARAD) of the US Department of Transportation (USDOT) and the US Army Corps of Engineers (USACE).

- MARAD is the USDOT agency responsible for America's waterborne transportation system, including IWT and other maritime functions.
- USACE is a federal agency under the US Department of Defense that primarily oversees dams, canals, and flood protection in the United States, as well as a wide range of public works throughout the world. USACE employs about 37,000 personnel— the majority are civil—who work on facilitating safe,

reliable, and economically efficient movement of IWT vessels. It does this by building and maintaining navigation channels and harbors, operating most locks, and regulating water levels on inland waterways. Its responsibilities in the IWT area are supported by the Institute for Water Resources (IWR), which was set up by USACE in 1969 to provide the USACE with long-range research and planning capabilities to assist in improving the civil works planning and evaluation process. IWR provides specialist expertise in hydrological engineering, integrated water resources management, international trends and experience, planning, policy analysis, and project management.

of Defense. This arrangement appears to work reasonably well with regard to efficiency of administration, and certainly for the coordinated management of the many water resource issues. IWT in the United States is unique because all of the other transport networks in America use civilian administrative models. One of the advantages of the US system is that the centralization allows for national planning and integrated development.

In China, the administration of much of the IWT system has been decentralized to provincial governments and this has created challenges to attaining consistent policies and coordinated actions. China's division of administration—where MoT, through specialized River Administrations, is responsible for the IWT infrastructure on the main waterways of the two most important rivers, the Yangtze and the Pearl, while provincial governments administer the rest of the IWT infrastructure through provincial navigation administrations—is logical and appropriate for China. However, this division of administration creates inconsistencies and a lack of harmony between provinces in the application and implementation of policies and standards in areas such as vessel licensing, environmental compliance, pricing, and cost recovery.

The European Union has a complex institutional mechanism for IWT governance (see box 3.3), which reflects the reality that the commercially significant waterways in Europe are international waterways subject to international rights, obligations, and institutional arrangements that have been defined by international agreements and treaties between sovereign nations for two centuries. The complexity of IWT governance in the European Union also reflects the reality that the nations with interests in IWT in Europe include both EU and non-EU member countries, which creates a further challenge for policy harmonization, technical regulation, and economic integration.

BOX 3.3

Managing IWT in the European Union

The IWT industry within the European Union is governed by the following four levels:

- Individual European national governments (usually by a country's Ministry of Transport or its national IWT agency).
- Multinational River Commissions established by international conventions; the two most important conventions are the 1868 Mannheim Convention on the Rhine River and its tributaries, and the 1948 Belgrade Convention on the Danube River and its tributaries.
- The European Union (EU) itself, established in 1957 by the Treaty of Rome.

- United Nations Economic Commission for Europe, which is not an administrative body (it has no powers of implementation) but seeks harmonization of IWT navigation and environmental standards across Europe (including EU and non-EU countries).

Before the European Union was created, the IWT sector in Europe was administered at the first two levels. However, the progressive widening of the membership and powers of the European Union has added a third level of policy making and administration of IWT for respective EU member states.

Introduction of central-to-local IWT management and shipping administration

In China, the reform of IWT was carried out as part of the national reform of China's economic system. The first step in the process was to better clarify the roles and responsibilities between central and provincial administrations—with more autonomy going to the provinces.

Transportation along the Yangtze River (Changjiang) was the focus of reform. The first step was to separate responsibilities for navigation and ports (table 3.3). In December 1983, the Yangtze River Administration of Navigational Affairs (CJHY) and the Changjiang National Shipping Corporation (CSC) were set up after unbundling the Changjiang National Shipping Company.[1] CJHY was responsible for the administration of navigation, ports, and waterway regulation along the trunk waterways of the Yangtze River. The navigation administration agencies in provinces along the Yangtze River were to be under its guidance and were to implement uniform rules, regulations, and instructions. The trunk waterways of the Yangtze River and the important tributaries to be developed by the central government were included in the national waterways system, and the central government was charged with planning and constructing them uniformly. The Yangtze Waterway Bureau (CJHDJ), subordinate to CJHY, was fully responsible for the construction and maintenance of the trunk waterways of the Yangtze River. Other tributaries were classified as provincial or prefectural waterways; they were to be planned and constructed by the provincial or prefectural authorities.

The second step in the reform process was to separate the administration and management responsibilities of CJHY. The management of ports was transferred to local governments while CJHY was in charge of administration and oversight of IWT on the Yangtze. Subsequently, similar reforms were carried out

TABLE 3.3 Roles and responsibilities of main navigation affairs in China

BUREAU	DESCRIPTION	RESPONSIBILITIES
Yangtze Navigation Affairs	Agency of the Ministry of Transport responsible for development, management, and administration of the Yangtze River trunk line	• Strategy development and planning • Provision of regulatory framework for Yangtze River trunk line navigation • Coordination of water resources and utilization • Coordination of port and shipping business in provinces and cities along Yangtze Basin • Infrastructure development, shoreline administration, management of fairways and navigational facilities • Management of navigational safety and security • Development of science and technology • Administration of navigation • Monitoring of inland transport market
Pearl River Navigation Affairs	Agency of the Ministry of Transport responsible for development, management, and administration of the Pearl River	• Strategy development and planning • Coordination of water resources and utilization • Infrastructure development, management of fairways, and navigational management • Administration of navigation • Monitoring of inland transport market
North Jiangsu Grand Canal Administration of Navigation Affairs	Subordinated organization of the Jiangsu Provincial Department of Transport	• Management of sections of the Grand Canal in North Jiangsu • Development and maintenance of infrastructure • Management of fairways and navigation facilities • Administration of navigation

Source: China Waterborne Transport Research Institute.

FIGURE 3.2

Institutional reform adds clarity to IWT responsibilities

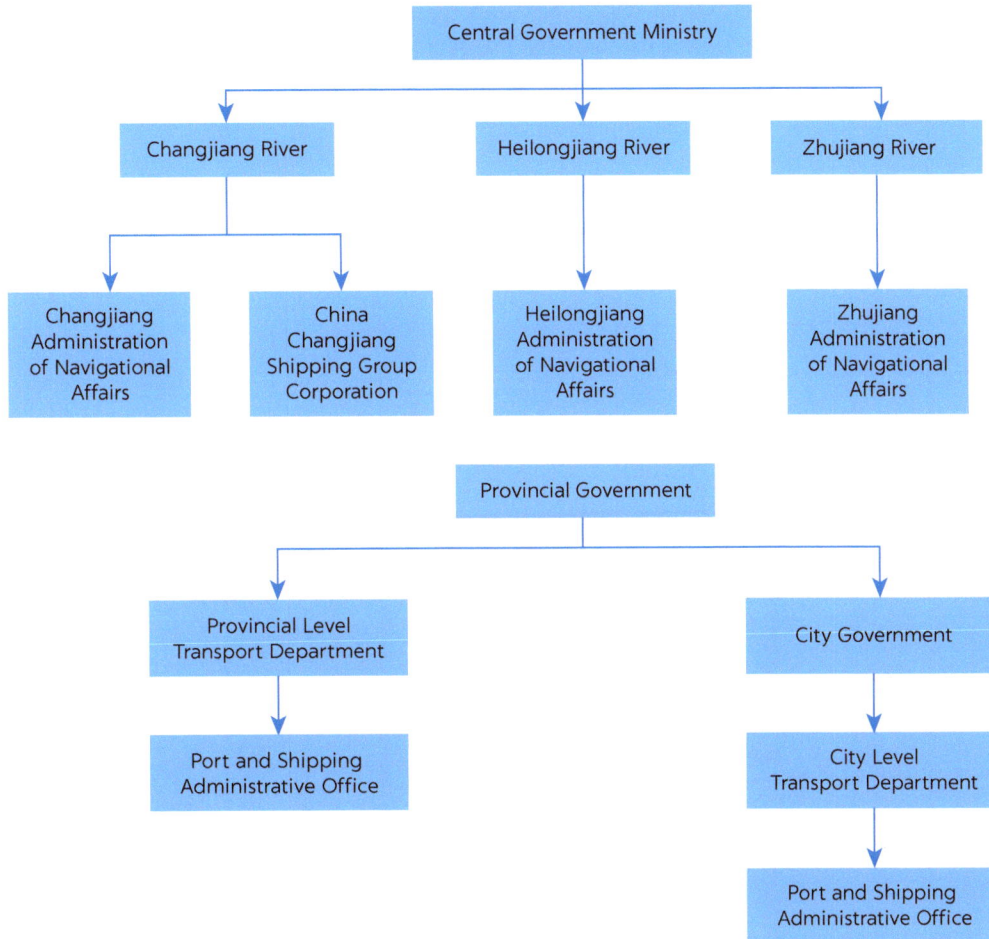

Source: World Bank creation.

on the other main river systems by forming semiautonomous entities for each river system (figure 3.2). In 1983, the Heilongjiang River Administration of Navigational Affairs was transferred from the province to the Ministry of Communications. In 1986, the Ministry of Transport set up the Pearl River Administration of Navigational Affairs (ZJHW). In November 1987, the Grand Canal Administration of North Jiangsu was set up, and this bureau took charge of the management of the Xuzhou-Yangzhou section of the Grand Canal. The Changjiang National Shipping Corporation continued to have a distinct role in managing ports.

Thus, a central-to-local management system of inland water navigation and transportation was formed, and the construction and management of inland water navigation and transportation were strengthened.

After the reforming of IWT institutions, clearer roles and responsibilities were established with respect to specific rivers; thus, the focus of reform shifted to trade management and macro control. Starting with the Changjiang River Administration of Navigational Affairs, the focus shifted to the institutional reform of river ports and the clear identification of the responsibilities for port and navigation authorities. On the basis of the separation of port management and navigation management and the identification of the responsibilities for port and navigation authorities, the State Council approved in August 1987 a "Request for Reform in Management System of Ports on the Changjiang River." It was decided that all of the ports on the main stream of the Changjiang River, except Zhangjiagang Port in Jiangsu Province, would be transferred to a lower level, and the principles of transfer and support policies were formulated. After consultation among the Ministry of Communications, the Changjiang River Administration of Navigational Affairs, and related provinces and cities, the preparation work of transfer was finished at the end of 1987, and the transfer was completed in 1988. After the transfer of the ports, the Changjiang River Administration of Navigational Affairs, as an agency of the Ministry of Communications, took charge of the administration of waterways, navigation, and trade management, and at the same time, it provided supervision, planning, coordination, and services.

In addition, the institutional reforms were accompanied by regulatory reforms:

- **Regulations for IWT management**: Detailed regulations also were prepared for safety, contracts for freight on waterways, local shipping enterprises, use of navigation channels, and waterway management.
- **Incentives for investments in IWT**: After a review of IWT shortfalls, preferential policies on taxation remission, freight rate readjustment, supply of diesel oil, and loans were released and piloted in the provinces of Jiangsu, Zhejiang, Jiangxi, Sichuan, Anhui, Fujian, Guangdong, Guangxi, and Hubei.
- **Local operational improvement**: Experiments were made at the operational level to determine how to unlock the potential of private enterprises and IWT users—especially self-employed individuals and small companies.

LONG-TERM COMPREHENSIVE PLANNING AND CONSTRUCTION OF INLAND WATERWAYS

IWT is considered the cleanest, safest, and most cost-efficient mode of hinterland transportation. To fully exploit those advantages, it is important to facilitate navigation on a nationwide scale. The basis of a nationwide system for safe, clean, and cost-efficient navigation is the waterway classification framework, which is used for barge standardization and upgrading. Related construction or maintenance of the IWT network is carefully planned and supported by (pre-) feasibility studies.

China has abundant inland rivers. About 80 percent of them cover at least 100,000 square kilometers and have navigation potential. To effectively use available resources and stimulate the national economy and social development, China crafted a long-term comprehensive inland navigational fairway network plan that considers the role of IWT in regional economic development, the comprehensive national transport system, the comprehensive use of water resources of all rivers, and national security. National IWT planning by the Ministry of Transport includes planning of all inland waterway grades and all types of inland ports. Special, dedicated plans are designed for fleet development, standardization, navigational aids, key projects, information technology (IT) systems, and safety and emergency response systems. National IWT studies are undertaken and several supportive pre-studies are usually conducted to inform decisions.

They are reviewed by local governments, state-owned enterprises, academic institutions, and related ministries.

Inland waterway surveys

Two major milestones were instrumental in collecting data on the navigability of China's inland waterways. In 1979 and in 2002, the Ministry of Transport conducted two national surveys of the IWT network to update the Chinese waterway classification system. The surveys inventoried about 180 key indicators, including waterway dimensions, river-crossing structures and riverside facilities, waterway hubs, and the waterway management and maintenance organization. The surveys enabled the establishment of a management information system (MIS) of national inland waterways and the preparation of an electronic atlas of national inland waterways. The waterway surveys provided accurate and reliable data for compiling the transport infrastructure construction plan and improving inland waterway management. Therefore, subsequent plans for development of IWT could be made on the basis of current and accurate information.

Classification of waterways and navigation standards

In the early stages of reform and opening up, major investments were made to safeguard the water supply and prevent flooding. The number of riverside and river-crossing structures increased, sometimes in violation of navigation standards. Problems developed because bridges were built too low for navigation and dams were constructed without locks. To counter this trend, the Ministry of Transport formulated standards for inland waterway navigation and classified waterways. The introduction of these construction, maintenance, and safeguard standards and their application to the entire waterway network provided a basis for accommodating China's shipping development, ensuring navigation safety, and realizing the standardized management of inland waterways. Photo 3.2 illustrates the need for increased attention to safety issues.

Classification of technical grade of waterways. In December 1990, the Ministry of Construction approved the implementation of inland waterway navigation standards. Inland waterways were to be classified into seven classes (or grades); plus, a category of substandard waterways and the dimensions and

PHOTO 3.2

Safety issues in IWT bring about safeguard standards

Source: © STC-NESTRA. Used with the permission of STC-NESTRA. Further permission required for reuse.

navigation tonnage standards for waterways with different classes were to be defined. This classification was adopted at a national conference on the management and maintenance of inland waterways in September 1992. In December 1994, the Ministry of Transport issued the "Work Outline for Technical Classification of Inland Waterways," which defined the objectives, tasks, and requirements for the classification of waterways and proposed applying the classification throughout the country. Transportation departments of all provinces (districts and cities) were to carry out their work under the unified deployment of the Ministry of Transport.

Classification of the inland waterways was completed by the end of 1999. For the approved waterway classes, 2030 was set as the target year to reach waterway grading for Classes I–IV; the target year for other classes was 2020. These classifications and clear development targets are the basis for planning and investments in waterway construction, upgrading, and management. The Waterway Management Department is to maintain and manage waterways in accordance with the waterway classification standards; it is obliged by law to prevent the construction of new structures that would obstruct navigation.

Formulation of inland waterway navigation aids and standards. In February 1986, the State Standards Bureau promulgated two national standards: "Aids to Navigation on Inland Waterways" and "Main Dimensions of Aids to Navigation on Inland Waterways." The Regulations of China for Navigation Aids (Decree No. 187, issued by the State Council in December 1995) is the first code of navigation aids officially promulgated and applicable to the introduction of navigational aids in Chinese waters and seas. Its purpose is to strengthen the management of and safeguard navigation aids, ensuring that navigational aids are in good condition. The regulations stipulate that the range of navigational aids to be under the management and protection of the transportation departments is all navigational aids except those used for military or fishery purposes. In May 1996, the Ministry of Transport further specified the management and organization involved in its Management Measures for Inland Waterway Navigation Aids (Decree No. 2). Management measures are to be based on more than 30 years of practical experience, including the use and promotion of new technologies in this field. The approach in this regulation is complete and systematic.

Restoring navigation through hydropower-cum-navigation complexes

In the early stages of reform and opening up, China's navigable inland rivers had 1,334 dams without navigation facilities. Through joint consultation, the Ministry of Transport and the Ministry of Water Resources and Electric Power strengthened organizational management and increased financial support to gradually restore the navigational function of waterways closed off by dams by designing and constructing navigation facilities.

In 1983, these ministries set up a coordination team. In January 1985, they decided that coordination teams composed of the water resources and electric power department and the transport department must be established in the provinces (districts and cities) that had dams without navigation facilities, to gradually resume navigation at such dams and to prevent the emergence of new dams without navigation facilities. In 1986, after the Ministry of Transport surveyed dams without navigation facilities, it formulated a plan for resuming

PHOTO 3.3
Construction of the Three Gorges dam and ship lock

Sources: © China Waterborne Transport Research Institute and STC-NESTRA. Used with the permission of China Waterborne Transport Research Institute and STC-NESTRA. Further permission required for reuse.

navigation through the approximately 150 dams for which economic value was demonstrated.

On the basis of the principle of "realizing self-development by relying on itself, creating a virtuous cycle, and producing benefits for all sides," the Ministry of Transport, in 1984, proposed that part of the revenue from power generated by the Three Gorges Dam power station should be used to fund flood control measures and the cascade of locks and thus ensure unimpeded navigation (photo 3.3). The construction of the double-way and five-step continuous ship locks of the Three Gorges project embodies the spirit of the comprehensive use of and the comprehensive benefits of water resources.

Infrastructure planning of the main network and tributaries

Because of IWT's principal role in the national economy, it is important for governments at all levels and waterway management departments to formulate scientifically justified, comprehensive, and feasible long-term development plans for IWT and for them to plan a phased development of the existing waterways to contribute to regional economic development.

The Ministry of Transport's "Outline of the Report on Modernization of Transportation," issued in March 1978, proposed the planning concepts for transportation through 2000. It proposed stepwise development of the Yangtze, Pearl, Huaihe, and other river basins and the completion of the Grand Canal and several other canals.

In October 1995, the Ministry of Transport defined the objectives, principles, and layout of China's core inland waterway corridors, which form the backbone of the national waterway network. These core waterway corridors form a network of 20 inland waterways, with a total length of about 15,000 kilometers, or about 14 percent of the total length of inland waterways in China. The network is called "one vertical route and three horizontal routes": one vertical route refers to the main channel of the Huaihe River of the Grand Canal and three horizontal routes refer to the main channel of the Yangtze River and its tributaries, the main channel of the Xijiang River and its tributaries, and the main channel of the Songhua River of the Heilongjiang River. At the national IWT conference in 1995 (see chapter 2), it was proposed that a pattern of "two horizontal routes, one vertical route, and two networks" be formed during the Ninth Five-Year Plan period (1996–2000).

In February 1998, the Ministry of Transport held a meeting on nationwide IWT development, confirming that in the decades to come, the main challenge for development of IWT was the realization of the two horizontal routes, one vertical route, and two networks, in which two horizontal routes refers to the main channels of the Yangtze River basin and the Pearl River basin, one vertical route refers to the main channel of the Grand Canal and the Huaihe River, and two networks refer to the waterway networks in the Yangtze River and Pearl River Deltas.

In line with China's western development strategy, in 2000 the Ministry of Transport issued the "Outline of Inland Waterway Transport Development in Western China." Its objectives for the first two decades were to form the main water transport network out of rivers and lakes in the western region, to improve the navigability of tributaries, and to develop port facilities up to Luzhou (photo 3.4) and a supporting service system for IWT. Realization of a modern IWT system was foreseen for the middle of the twenty-first century. The system would have waterways as its backbone and connect to tributaries. It would be an integral part of a multimodal transport system that would be equipped with modern technology and would provide high-quality services.

China's twenty-first century IWT policy is to gradually realize the long-term plan of "three main nodes and one supporting safeguard system" (a main highway framework, a main water transport channel, a main hub of ports and stations, and a traffic-supporting safeguard system). In 2004–05, the Ministry of Transport issued the "Plan (Key Points) for High-Class Waterway Network in the Yangtze River Delta" and the "Plan (Key Points) for High-Class Waterway Network in the Pearl River Delta." These two plans determine the projects needed to realize the core and backbone roles of those networks before 2010 and 2020, respectively. Because freight transport is expected to more than double between 2010 and 2020, the projects include smaller waterways that must be revitalized to meet the expected increase (photo 3.5).

PHOTO 3.4
Construction of Luzhou port

Source: © STC-NESTRA. Used with the permission of STC-NESTRA. Further permission required for reuse.

PHOTO 3.5
Current state of small waterways in China

Source: © China Waterborne Transport Research Institute. Used with the permission of China Waterborne Transport Research Institute. Further permission required for reuse.

The details of the plans by the Ministry of Transport are as follows:

1. For the layout plan of the Yangtze River Delta—with the Yangtze River trunk waterway and the Grand Canal as the core, the Class III waterways as the main body, and the Class IV waterways as a supplement—a high-grade waterway network with "two vertical routes and six horizontal routes" is formed by 23 waterways in the Yangtze River Delta. The focus of the plan is the construction of the inland container transport channels that lead to the main container port areas of the Shanghai International Shipping Center. The planned waterway mileage is 4,330 kilometers, including 3,400 kilometers of Class III and above waterways and 930 kilometers of Class IV waterways.

2. For the layout plan of the Pearl River Delta—with the Class III waterways as the base—a high-grade waterway network with "three vertical routes, three horizontal routes and three lines" is formed by 16 waterways. The planned waterway mileage is 939 kilometers.

3. IWT development in the western region is phase-driven. The first phase is the construction of main water transport channels to strengthen the construction of the Yangtze River trunk waterway, the Xijiang River trunk waterway, the Jialing River, the Hanjiang River, the Youjiang River, the Beipan River, the Hongshui River, and so forth, for a total waterway length of 4,060 kilometers. The second phase is the construction of and the connection of important tributaries of the main water transport channels, including the Qujiang, Wujiang, and Minjiang rivers of the Yangtze River basin and the Nanpan, Zuojiang, and Lancang rivers of the Pearl River basin (photo 3.6). The total length of the waterways is 2,545 kilometers. The third phase is the construction of navigation facilities in sectional navigable rivers (river reaches) and reservoirs (lakes) with obvious benefits, such as those in reservoirs and lakes of the Jinsha and Yellow rivers, to meet the increasing demand for tourism and to meet the demand for transportation in the remote western regions.

Phased implementation of planning objectives

From 1981 to 1990, the focus of waterway construction was on dredging and maintenance to keep the main channel unimpeded. With a focus on the Yangtze,

PHOTO 3.6
Development of tributary waterways

Sources: © China Waterborne Transport Research Institute and STC-NESTRA. Used with the permission of China Waterborne Transport Research Institute and STC-NESTRA. Further permission required for reuse.

Xijiang, Heilongjiang, and Huaihe rivers and the Grand Canal, IWT development sought to improve the navigation conditions of main tributaries to resolve the existence of dams without planned navigation facilities, to increase the mileage of navigable waterways to 7,000 kilometers for barge fleets of more than 1,000 tons, and to increase gradually the modal share of IWT. In 1982, the central government renovated the northern Jiangsu section of the Grand Canal, dredged and widened the waterway, and constructed double-line ship locks. With the approval of the State Council, the northern Jiangsu section of the Grand Canal was classified as a Class III national inland waterway and included in the national construction plan, according to the "Project Plan and Assignment Book of the Xijiang River Navigation Construction" (Ministry of Transport 1978b). In 1988, the Gezhouba Dam Water Conservancy Project was completed; the Ministry of Transport and the Ministry of Water Resources coordinated the resumption of some dams without navigation facilities. And, in 1989, the central government completed the first phase of the Xiangjiang River navigation construction project (a 1,000-ton waterway with a length of 257 kilometers from Chenglingji to Zhuzhou).

From 1991 to 2000, the focus was on the construction of IWT infrastructure to improve the waterway grade. The principal water transport channel of the main streams of the Yangtze River, the Xijiang River, and the Grand Canal (Jining–Hangzhou) was formed (see photo 3.7), and the inland waterway pattern, with a connection between the southern Yangtze River waterway network in the Yangtze River Delta and the waterway network in the Pearl River Delta, took shape. During the Ninth Five-Year Plan period (1996–2000), investment in the construction of the inland waterway gradually increased. As a result,

PHOTO 3.7
Traffic on the Grand Canal

Source: © STC-NESTRA. Used with the permission of STC-NESTRA. Further permission required for reuse.

additional waterway construction to create high-grade waterway networks took place, including phase II of the Xiangjiang River (Zhuzhou–Hengyang) navigation construction project, the extension project of the Jining–Taierzhuang section of the Grand Canal, the reconstruction and expansion project of the Sunan Canal, and the construction of the Zhejiang section of the Grand Canal.

From 2000 to 2010, the focus of construction was on improving waterways to the sea, improving the navigation conditions of inland waterways, constructing the Yangtze River Golden Waterway and the high-grade waterway network in the Yangtze River Delta, and promoting combined river-sea transportation. The following objectives were to be achieved by 2010:

- Conditions of the Yangtze River trunk waterways are significantly improved
- 50,000-ton ships can sail directly to Nanjing
- 3,000-ton ships can sail seasonally to Chenglingji, in Hunan Province
- The 10,000-ton fleet in the Three Gorges Reservoir Region can sail directly to the main ports of Chongqing
- 1,000-ton ships can sail directly to Shuifu, in Yunnan Province
- The main waterways in the high-grade waterway network in the Yangtze River Delta are navigable by 1,000-ton ships
- Shipping congestion in the Grand Canal is significantly reduced

The main framework of the high-grade waterway network in the Pearl River Delta was formed first, with consideration of the requirements of container transportation and the rapid economic and social development within the region.

Since 2010, several major inland waterway projects have been built. In September 2014, the State Council prepared the plan for the multimodal transport corridor of the Yangtze River Economic Belt (2014–20) to comprehensively promote the systematic management of the Yangtze River trunk waterways.

The plan proposed to further improve navigation capacity in the following waterways:

- In the downstream section of the Yangtze River, the 12.5-meter deep-water waterway will be extended to Nanjing.
- In the midstream section of the Yangtze River, a project for regulating the waterway at the Jingjiang River section will be carried out and priority given to model tests for the waterway from Yichang to Anqing.
- In the upstream section of the Yangtze River, the Chongqing–Yibin waterway regulation project will be carried out and the Yibin–Shuifu waterway regulation project will be studied and tested.
- The potential of ship locks at the Three Gorges Dam will be tapped by upgrading current infrastructure and facilities (photo 3.8). The capacity expansion project of the ship locks of the Three Gorges and Gezhouba dams and the regulation project of the waterway between them will be launched.
- Construction of branches and tributaries will be promoted in a coordinated manner.

PHOTO 3.8

The Three Gorges ship lock and ship lift

Source: © STC-NESTRA. Used with the permission of STC-NESTRA. Further permission required for reuse.

- Construction of high-grade waterways—including the Hefei–Yuxikou water-way; waterways on the Xinjiang, Ganjiang, Hanjiang, Yuanshui, Xiangjiang, Wujiang, and Minjiang rivers; and the Jianghan Canal—will be accelerated.
- Waterway construction of the Grand Canal and capacity expansion of ship locks will be carried out.
- The high-grade waterway network in the Yangtze River Delta will be constructed systematically.

FUNDING FOR INLAND WATERWAY TRANSPORT INFRASTRUCTURE IN CHINA

Upgrading China's IWT infrastructure required enormous investments in waterways, ports, logistics zones, supporting systems (such as river information services), the emergency response system, and traffic management systems. It also involved upgrading IWT operations, including the vessel fleet and the skills of staff and crew, which could not have been realized without major investments and support programs. Figure 3.3 shows an overview of the funding for IWT development, which the following subsections discuss.

Reforms in financing inland waterways

Inland waterways are public property and as such offer socioeconomic benefits. To ensure those benefits, the government has implemented various investments in IWT.

In the early stage of reform and opening up, the central government allocated a certain amount of funds in the plan each year to subsidize local projects for the construction of inland waterways and for other waterway functions, such as agriculture. But massive waterway development required huge amounts of capital for construction and maintenance, and the shortage of funds for waterways has long been a main constraint on development of the waterway industry. IWT reforms have included measures and preferential policies that have promoted investment and financing, including opening new financing channels, raising additional local funds, and attracting foreign investment.

FIGURE 3.3

Funding sources for development of inland waterway transport in China

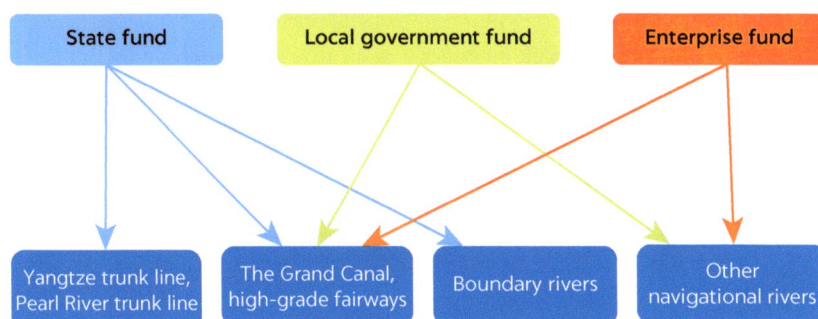

Source: China Waterborne Transport Research Institute data.

Since the Eighth Five-Year Plan (1991–95), a combination of central and regional financing systems has been in place to facilitate inland waterway projects of national and regional importance. During the Ninth Five-Year Plan period (1996–2000), the central government created a dedicated fund for building inland waterway infrastructure and supporting systems that was funded by motor vehicle purchase surcharges.

Reform of IWT development explored and opened several avenues for financing projects, including the following:

- State (central and local) budgetary funds
- Dedicated funds of the Ministry of Transport (the vehicle purchase tax, the port construction fee, and special expenditure allocations for inland waterways)
- Loans by domestic banks (mainly policy banks)
- Foreign capital
- Local self-raised funds
- Funds of enterprises and institutions

Multichannel fundraising opportunities also have been explored and exploited at the provincial and lower levels of government. These opportunities have formulated preferential policies and have created financing models such as power generation for navigation, which has promoted the combination of navigation development and power generation as a financing tool. In respective projects, navigation locks and facilities were built alongside micropower generation facilities. Where conditions were favorable, multiparty investments were made to fund navigation-power solutions on the basis of shared investment, risks, and profits. For this purpose, concession models were offered to financial organizations and governments. Large industrial complexes, mines, and enterprises also were encouraged to participate in building waterway facilities under the overall planning of the competent administrative department for transportation. The benefits of these multidisciplinary projects were distributed on the basis of each party's investment. Recently, local government investment platforms have been set up in some places to invest in inland waterway construction.

Local government IWT funds. China adopted the hierarchical management model at the central and local levels. In this model, central government authorities are responsible for maintaining navigation aids and lighthouses in the trunk waterways of the Yangtze and Heilongjiang rivers and the public coastal trunk waterways; local authorities are responsible for maintaining waterways and navigation aids within their jurisdictions. The main sources of waterway maintenance funds are waterway maintenance fees, enterprise income, local financial subsidies, other shipping fees, and port charges for cargo. Box 3.4 gives an example of the development of a dedicated IWT program by the local government of Chongqing.

Strengthening the collection of waterway-related fees. The main sources of funds for waterway management and maintenance are waterway maintenance fees and ship-lockage fees. In August 1992, the Ministry of Transport, the Ministry of Finance, and the State Price Control Bureau jointly issued "Measures for the Collection and Use of Maintenance Fees for Inland Waterways." It clarified the scope of collection of waterway maintenance fees, adjusted the collection standard, specified that waterway maintenance fees be collected and managed by the waterway management organizations under the transportation

BOX 3.4

Development of inland water transport in Chongqing

Chongqing—a city of 31 million inhabitants located about 2,200 kilometers from Shanghai, at the mouth of the Yangtze—is the inland shipping center of southwest China. The city has waterway resources. The Yangtze trunk line crosses the city from its west to its east; the Jialingjiang, a tributary of the Yangtze, crosses the Yangtze in Chongqing; and the city has other small rivers. Chongqing has about 4,400 kilometers of navigable waterways, of which 1,400 kilometers are classified greater than Class IV. Total cargo throughput at Chongqing ports reached 204 million tons and 1.2 million 20-foot equivalent units (TEUs) of containers in 2018.

IWT investment in Chongqing is funded from several resources. The national government has invested in the section of the Yangtze trunk line across Chongqing and Jialingjiang, which is part of the 2-1-2-18 network. This investment went toward dredging, maintenance, information and communication technology, safety, and security management. Chongqing's local government is responsible for raising investment funds for IWT for all sections in its jurisdiction. The Chongqing local government has allocated funds to develop IWT infrastructure, support port construction, stimulate inland shipping industry, and set up government agencies to help build the capacity of the IWT industry. It also established a public corporation that serves as both an investment platform and as an operational body for the construction and operation of transport infrastructure.

departments at various levels, and strengthened the management of the use of waterway maintenance fees.

Establishing dedicated funds for the development of inland waterway transport. Under the Ninth Five-Year Plan period (1996–2000), the central government established dedicated funds for IWT development by using construction funds for key energy and transportation projects and reconciling funds for the national budget. The central government decreed that such dedicated funds should be arranged uniformly by the Ministry of Transport for the construction of water transport infrastructure. Since then, the Ministry of Transport has allocated part of the dedicated funds from the vehicle purchase tax and port construction fee to waterway construction and IWT development. In 2005–07, it invested ¥1–¥1.5 billion (about US$150–US$200 million) a year in inland waterway construction. Beginning in 2008, annual investment rose to about ¥2 billion (about US$300 million). In 2018, the Ministry of Transport invested more than ¥10.9 billion (US$1.5 billion) in dedicated funds for inland waterway construction; local governments raised about ¥8.1 billion (US$1.14 billion).

Using foreign capital and expertise. Since the Ninth Five-Year Plan period (1996–2000), international financing institutions have been providing loans for the construction of inland waterways. Foreign investment in such construction accumulated to about ¥7 billion (US$1 billion) until 2018. Inland waterway regulation and navigation-power junction projects in Guangdong, Guangxi, Hunan, Hubei, Jiangsu, Zhejiang, Jiangxi and other provinces were completed with loans from the World Bank or the Asian Development Bank. The use of loans from international financial institutions not only accelerated the realization of IWT infrastructure projects in China but also promoted the standardization and modernization of inland waterway management. The World Bank, the Asian Development Bank, and other international financial organizations carried out project management for the entire project life cycle and introduced standardized systems and practices that consisted of project preparatory work, project implementation (including bidding and tendering management), and postproject evaluation to ensure smooth implementation of projects. The introduction of advanced international management concepts and experiences played an important role in bringing China's inland waterway construction and maintenance management in line with the rest of the world.

For 25 years, the World Bank has been involved in IWT projects in China (see box 3.5).

As stated by the minister of Qian Yongchang at the National Transportation Conference in 1985, the policy of "all departments, industries, and regions

BOX 3.5

The World Bank and China: A 25-year partnership in IWT development

Beginning with the first inland waterway project in 1995, the World Bank has supported eight inland waterway projects in China. Each successive phase of inland waterway transport (IWT) development in China has introduced important additionality, ranging from technical innovation to integrated development and management of multipurpose inland waterway transport, as well as improved institutional capacity and environmental aspects.

During the course of China's opening up and economic transformation, the World Bank played a catalytic role and supported China in building world-class IWT infrastructure, upgrading and modernizing river and canal networks, and developing integrated transport corridors for improving regional connectivity and productivity.

The objectives of the first IWT projects were to provide more efficient and productive IWT services that would be more competitive than the existing services. This would be achieved through the reduction of unit cost and transit time by upgrading inland waterway infrastructure to allow navigation of larger-size vessels, increasing ship-lock capacity to reduce waiting time, and increasing financial and organizational capacity of IWT agencies.

The World Bank's IWT projects were carried out in the inland provinces of China (among others, in Hunan, Guangxi, Zhejiang, Jiangxi, Guangdong, Hubei, and Anhui) on the tributaries of the trunk waterways of the Yangtze and the Pearl River Delta.

An important element in most of the projects was the construction of hydropower-cum-navigation complexes on smaller waterways. The construction of a dam, hydropower plant, and ship lock proved to be an innovative way of combining different uses of the waterway in a sustainable manner:

- Improved navigation conditions (stable channel, guaranteed and increased draft, higher class, increased reliability)
- Supply of renewable energy
- Gravity flow irrigation to farmland
- Flood risk mitigation
- Economic development along the waterway
- Reducing economic disparities between coastal and inland areas
- Ecological improvement via greener transport
- Smart financing mechanism for infrastructure improvement via hydropower sales

In addition to infrastructure reform, institutional and financial reforms were introduced to pilot provinces; staff training programs for capacity building were provided through World Bank loans and technical assistance.

Although currently there are concerns about the adverse effects of the construction of dams in waterways on the environment and ecology, from a financial perspective, these multifunctional complexes were successful, and the navigability of the waterways has been improved significantly.

The World Bank's lending to China's IWT projects continuously demonstrates innovation. The new era of IWT development in China requires the adoption of an integrated, multimodal approach that takes into account the challenges of multiple users of waterways and the impact of climate change. An example of this new project approach is provided in chapter 4.

working together, [and] all state-owned, collectively owned enterprises and individuals cooperating together, to make use of all means of transport" has produced a variety of successes. The role of the central government is to formulate and implement policies and measures and to encourage and support parties that invest in waterway construction. For local waterway construction, third parties are engaged in multilevel and multichannel funding mechanisms to provide capital. Examples of these funding channels include loans from policy banks (banks in China that finance economic and trade development and state-invested projects), commercial banks, allocation of government funds, establishment of investment platforms, and direct investment by enterprises. Examples of regional initiatives include the following:

- Every year, the government of Guangdong Province allocates ¥200 million (about US$70 million) for waterway construction and maintenance, which is a large share of waterway-related work in the province.
- Hubei Province has allocated ¥100 million (about US$15 million) a year for IWT development since 2006.
- The Chongqing Municipal Government has set up a ship-financing guarantee fund to provide guarantees for small and medium inland waterway shipping enterprises to purchase ships.
- In Gansu, Jilin, and other provinces, basic expenditures for waterway maintenance and management have been included in provincial budgets.
- The provincial financial departments of Guizhou Province and Yunnan Province subsidize waterway maintenance and management. Some county-level governments also have provided funds and other active support for waterway maintenance.
- The central government allows the establishment of specific IWT companies that are responsible for the financing, operational management, asset management, and loan repayment of IWT projects. In Anhui, Jiangxi, Hunan, and other provinces, for example, port and waterway investment and development groups have been established. They are responsible for the investment and financing, construction, and operational management of IWT infrastructure.
- The Ministry of Transport supports government departments and related enterprises in the provinces (districts and cities) that have raised funds for the joint development of IWT. For example, Zhejiang Province has 14 trunk waterways with a total length of 1,100 kilometers (10 percent of the total length in this province); they are approved as "four-self waterway projects" (self-financing, self-construction, self-charging, and self-repayment). Regulation allows for toll periods for waterways of up to 30 years. The charging standard is ¥1–¥5 (about US$0.15–US$0.75) per deadweight ton vessel capacity.
- It is encouraged to canalize waterways by constructing dams with both power generation and navigation facilities. Revenue from power generation can be used for further waterway improvements.
- Investors in the construction of inland ports and waterways are allowed to carry out comprehensive land development through land reclamation, with the proceeds used for IWT development. The compensation fees for any damage to or occupation of waterways and revetments and the maintenance funds reserved for construction projects must be used for the restoration, construction, and maintenance of waterway facilities.

Reforms in financing inland ports

Since the separation of government function from enterprise management in the port industry, the central government has implemented a policy of diversified sources of investment. The regulations of the Port Act encourage domestic and foreign economic organizations and individuals to invest in and operate ports. The relevant governments at or above the county level are supposed to ensure the necessary capital investment in the construction and maintenance of public waterways, breakwaters, anchorages, and other infrastructure at ports. In addition, they must take measures to organize the construction of ancillary facilities of ports—such as waterways, railways, highways, water supply and drainage, and power supply and communication—and to provide legislative guarantees for the construction of the public infrastructure of ports.

The financial position of most public inland port terminals is weak, and it is difficult to absorb private capital. Therefore, construction is organized and financed mainly by local governments. The central government provides capital subsidies to inland port terminals that are included in the Ministry of Transport's construction plan. The main source of this subsidy is the central government's share of the port construction fee. During the 12th Five-Year Plan period (2011–15), the central government's share of port construction fees was dedicated mainly to the improvement of waterways, ship locks, ship lifts, and navigation-power junctions and to the construction of inland ports in the central and western regions (see photo 3.9 for examples of new inland port development).

After 40 years of reform and opening up, China has established a port investment and financing system. The collection of port construction fees has become an important funding source that ensures smooth port construction in China. The Chinese government also encourages the participation of private capital and foreign capital in port construction.

The Ministry of Transport's encouragement of private sector engagement has attracted the participation of various entities such as industrial and

PHOTO 3.9

New ports and terminals in the Grand Canal and Han River

Source: © STC-NESTRA. Used with the permission of STC-NESTRA. Further permission required for reuse.
Note: Picture on the left is of the Grand Canal; picture on the right is of the Han River.

MAP 3.1

MAP 3.1

Emergence of institutional cooperation among sea and river ports in Northwestern Europe

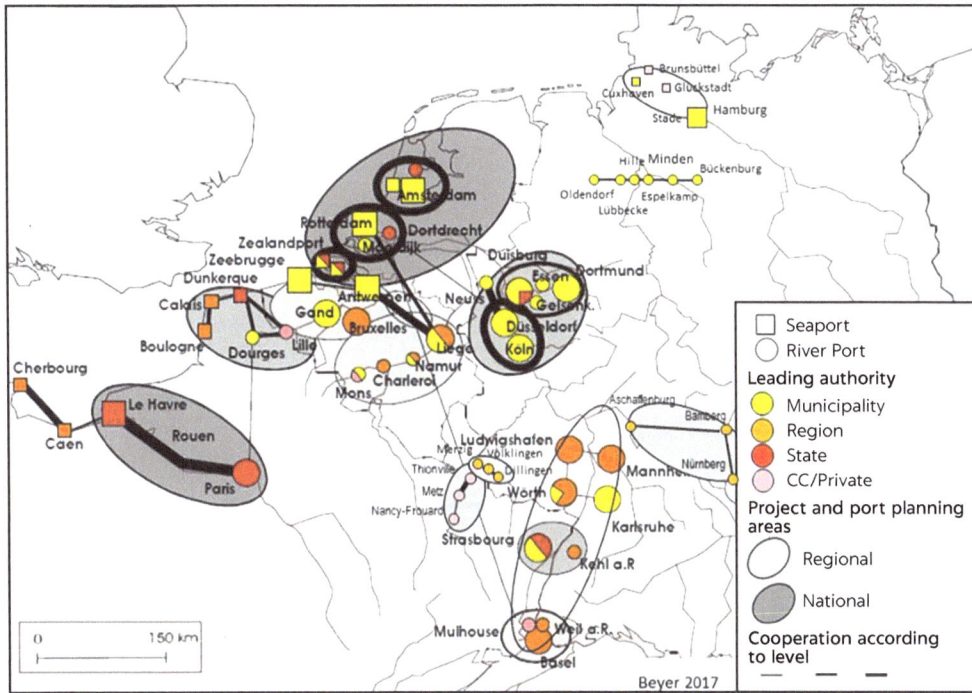

Source: Beyer 2018.

mining enterprises, material supply departments, and shipping companies. These enterprises have invested in the construction of terminals, while coal, iron, steel, chemical, and grain enterprises have built specialized wharfs for cargo owners in coastal and riverside areas.

An important effect of port reform is the integration of ports; for example, the investments from Shanghai International Port Group (SIPG) in a number of river ports, followed by a streamlining and upgrading of IWT port operations. Port integration along corridors is an international trend (see map 3.1).

FLEET UPGRADING THROUGH THE BARGE STANDARDIZATION PROGRAM

Before China launched its barge standardization program, the average age of the fleet was more than 30 years, capacity was low, and vessels were not designed for the new and improved waterways. In general, waterway transportation was not efficient or competitive, despite investments in navigation infrastructure.

Classifying waterways opened the way for the classification and standardization of the fleet. Barge standardization was seen as a strategic measure to upgrade the fleet, which would increase transport capacity (per vessel and for the fleet as a whole) and remove obsolete vessels from the market.

TABLE 3.4 **Barge standardization programs in China, 2003–15**

PERIOD	MAIN ACTIVITIES
2003–07	A standardization program for the Grand Canal was initiated. The Ministry of Transport, jointly with provincial governments along the Grand Canal, issued a detailed implementation plan. Incentives of more than ¥1 billion (about US$150 million) led to the scrapping of more than 40,000 old vessels.
2006–13	The Ministry of Transport issued the "National Barge Standardization Outline," which set objectives for 2010 and 2020 for the areas upstream of the Three Gorges Dam as well as the Yangtze trunk line, the Grand Canal, the Pearl River Delta, and the Pearl River trunk line. In 2009, an innovative policy for the Yangtze trunk line barge standardization was issued, with funding of ¥2 billion (about US$300 million).
2013–15	The barge standardization program was strengthened at the national level. In 2013, the Ministry of Transport issued an implementation plan that promoted barge standardization at the national level, which specified vessel designs along the 2-1-2-18 high-grade networks. The implementation plan set a goal of having standardized barges account for 50 percent of the total fleet on the 2-1-2-18 network and for 70 percent of all barges operating on the Yangtze, Pearl, and the Grand Canal.

Source: China Waterborne Transport Research Institute data.

Overview of barge standardization programs

In the early 2000s, the Ministry of Transport initiated a series of barge standardization measures. Table 3.4 provides an overview of the programs implemented between 2003 and 2015.

In some segments of the market, upgrading of the inland vessel fleet has lagged behind the massive increases in IWT volumes in recent decades. For example, on the Grand Canal at the end of the twentieth century, more than 40 percent of inland vessels were motor vessels of up to a few hundred tons with outboard (hanging-paddle) engines. These vessels have low transport efficiency, are noisy, pollute the water, are often involved in accidents, and create heavy congestion on the Grand Canal. The rapid growth of transport volumes and the future prospects of inland waterways provide a historical opportunity to reverse this situation and modernize the fleet. And the key approach to do so in China is barge standardization.

A series of barge standardization projects were carried out for the Grand Canal in 2003. Those projects were followed by projects in the Chuanjiang River and the Three Gorges Reservoir region in 2006 and the Yangtze River trunk waterway in 2009.

National barge standardization

In 2006, the Ministry of Transport issued an "Outline of Development of Barge Standardization" to guide national barge standardization and to establish a long-term mechanism to promote national barge standardization. It stipulated that barge standardization would be realized in the Chuanjiang River, the Three Gorges Reservoir region, the Grand Canal, the Yangtze River, and the Pearl River Delta and its main streams by 2010. The outline indicated that by 2010 the average tonnage should be double that of the average tonnage of 2004 and that vessel safety and technical performance should be further improved. Barge standardization was to be completed by 2020, by which time average tonnage should be three times the 2004 level and vessel safety and technical performance should approach internationally advanced levels.

The Ministry of Transport formulated a series of supporting measures in the form of organizational, institutional, and economic incentives and funding guarantees. A subsidy (compensation) mechanism was established that specified the subsidy fund channels, standards, and targets and ensured that subsidies were correctly applied. At the same time, the ministry adopted measures on the collection of fees and priorities in ship-lockage. The administrative and economic measures encourage and promote the standardization of vessels: the central and local governments provide financial support for the promotion of barge standardization and for the research and development (R&D) of standardized vessels; local governments provide financial support for the withdrawal of outmoded vessels from the market.

To implement the 12th Five-Year Plan (2011–15) and focus on promoting barge standardization in line with the 2-1-2-18 plan, barge standardization was promoted nationwide, new nonstandard vessels were strictly prohibited from entering the shipping market, and old and energy-consuming vessels were encouraged to exit the shipping market ahead of schedule. The implementation plan aimed at achieving a barge standardization rate of more than 50 percent of total tonnage of the total fleet and 70 percent of the fleet operating on the Yangtze River trunk waterway, the Xijiang River trunk waterway, and the Grand Canal.

The implementation plan also stated that (a) port and waterway departments shall not handle operation procedures for new nonstandardized vessels and vessels to be withdrawn from the market within a specified period; (b) the maritime department shall not handle the registration procedures for new nonstandardized vessels or issue certificates for vessels to be withdrawn from the market within a specified period; (c) the ship inspection department shall not accept the inspection of the construction of nonstandardized vessels; and (d) the ship-lock administration department shall not arrange lockage for vessels that are prohibited from lockage or vessels that will withdraw from the market within a specified period. This combination of strong regulations and signals to the market were critical to making the standardization a reality.

Barge standardization for the Yangtze

The development of the fleet in the Yangtze River basin did not keep pace with other investments or the increase in transport demand. State investment had achieved remarkable improvements in infrastructure and ports in the basin. However, vessels still had small average tonnage and many were in poor condition and were equipped with outdated technology—there was an urgent need to improve the competitiveness and the safety of navigation on the Yangtze River. A modernized fleet would increase the capacity of the Three Gorges ship lock, improve navigation safety in the reservoir area, and reduce pollution by vessels.

To accelerate barge standardization for the Yangtze River trunk waterway, the Ministry of Transport and the Ministry of Finance—together with the governments of Shanghai and Chongqing, and the provinces of Jiangsu, Anhui, Jiangxi, Hubei, Hunan, Sichuan, Yunnan, and Henan—formulated and issued the "Implementation Plan for Promoting the Barge Standardization for the Yangtze River Trunk Waterway," which came into force October 1, 2009. The plan proposed that by December 1, 2013, the barge standardization rate of the Chuanjiang River and the Three Gorges Reservoir region should exceed 75 percent, the handling capacity of the Three Gorges ship lock should increase by more than 10 percent, the average tonnage of cargo vessels in the Yangtze River trunk waterway should be more than 1,000 deadweight tons, and the safety and technical performance of vessels should be significantly improved (photo 3.10). When the plan was proposed, the most important reason for promoting barge standardization on the Yangtze River trunk waterway was to improve the handling capacity of the Three Gorges ship lock by increasing vessel size, improving vessels' technical standards and performance, and making vessels safer and more environmentally friendly.

Departments adopted various policies to promote barge standardization for the Yangtze River trunk waterway, in accordance with regional characteristics. The Ministry of Finance, the Ministry of Transport, and local governments raised dedicated funds and formulated economic incentive policies for the renovation, transformation, and elimination of existing vessels. To standardize the management of subsidy funds, "Measures for the Management of Subsidy Funds for Barge Standardization for the Yangtze River Trunk Waterway" (Ministry of Transport and Ministry of Finance 2009b) were formulated. The measures stipulated that between October 1, 2009, and December 31, 2013, central and local governments should each provide half of the subsidy for disassembling small-tonnage vessels of the Three Gorges ship lock, for disassembling old inland vessels of the Yangtze River trunk waterway and replacing them with new vessels (photo 3.11), for installing sewage treatment systems on existing passenger ships in the Three Gorges Reservoir region, and for reconstructing or disassembling single-hull oil tankers and single-hull chemical tankers in the Three Gorges Reservoir

PHOTO 3.10

New, standardized carrier for 871 cars suited for the Three Gorges reservoir and ship lock

Source: © Shanghai Ansheng Automotive Shipping Co., Ltd. Used with the permission of Shanghai Ansheng Automotive Shipping Co., Ltd. Further permission required for reuse.

PHOTO 3.11

New, standardized carrier for 800 cars suited for the Three Gorges ship lift

Source: © Shanghai Ansheng Automotive Shipping Co., Ltd. Used with the permission of Shanghai Ansheng Automotive Shipping Co., Ltd. Further permission required for reuse.

region. By the end of the policy implementation, ¥1.6 billion (about US$230 million) of government subsidies had been provided and more than 7,700 vessels had been approved for disassembling and reconstruction.

Barge standardization project for the Grand Canal

In 2003, the Ministry of Transport launched the barge standardization demonstration project for the Grand Canal. The project's purpose was to endorse recommended technical improvements to previous barge standards in industry regulations. The new regulations were vigorously promoted by various means, such as administration, regulations, and economic incentive policies to realize the rapid development and improvement of inland vessels.

On December 15, 2003, the central government issued the "Action Plan for Barge Standardization Demonstration Project of the Grand Canal" (Ministry of Transport 2003), which proposed banning all hanging-paddle motor vessels from the Grand Canal beginning January 1, 2007. The action plan was jointly issued by the Ministry of Transport and the governments of Shandong, Jiangsu, Zhejiang, Henan, Anhui, and Shanghai. For the smooth market exit of the more than 40,000 hanging-paddle motor vessels, those governments decided on a scheme of providing subsidies to owners that scrapped or modernized their hanging-paddle motor vessels ahead of schedule. This step marked the first time in the history of IWT in China that the IWT fleet was restructured by means of financial subsidies; it was an important demonstration for promoting barge standardization in other water basins. The central and local financial departments provided subsidies of ¥1 billion (about US$150 million). Those subsidies led to the withdrawal of about 40,000 hanging-paddle motor vessels on the Grand Canal ahead of schedule, completely changing the shipping market there and greatly improving ship navigation (photo 3.12). The withdrawal significantly reduced noise and water pollution, facilitated the structural adjustment of the transport capacity of the Grand Canal, and produced remarkable economic and social benefits.

PHOTO 3.12
Old vessels scrapped and new, standard vessels built under China's barge standardization program

Source: © STC-NESTRA. Used with the permission of STC-NESTRA. Further permission required for reuse.

Incentive policies and funding for barge standardization

The massive barge standardization programs could not have been realized in such a short period without support programs from the governments at different levels. In addition to the general measures and support described in the previous sections, the following measures were taken:

- *Yangtze trunk waterway scheme:* A fund of ¥2 billion (about US$300 million) was set up by the central and local governments to subsidize the disassembling and reconstruction of small-tonnage vessels passing through the Three Gorges ship lock, of passenger ships and roll-on/roll-off ships for trucks in the Three Gorges Reservoir region that failed to meet the requirements for domestic sewage discharge, of single-hull oil tankers and single-hull chemical tankers, and of old transport vessels of the Yangtze River trunk waterway.

- *Grand Canal scheme:* Barge owners of hanging-paddle motor vessels that choose to disassemble and scrap, to reconstruct the cabin, or to remove the outboard motor to transform their vessels into barges could apply for government subsidies (half from the central government, half from the local government).

- *National subsidy fund:* During the 12th Five-Year Plan period (2011–15), the economic incentive policy for national barge standardization included subsidy funds for national barge standardization. Subsidies were granted for the disassembling and reconstruction of (small) inland vessels and the installation of waste treatment systems on existing vessels, according to national technical standards. Old IWT vessels to be scrapped between October 2013 and December 2015 were given a subsidy of ¥1,000 (about US$150) per gross ton. The central government also provided subsidies for four other types of vessels, including new-model inland vessels. Subsidy funds for national barge standardization are arranged by the central and local financial departments through the public financial budget. The subsidies for the disassembling and reconstruction of existing vessels and the subsidies for the construction of new-model vessels of shipping enterprises owned by the central government (including holding subsidiaries) were to be fully borne by the central financial department. Subsidies for the disassembling and reconstruction of other vessels were to be shared by the central and local financial governments, in a ratio of 50:50 in the eastern provinces, 60:40 in the central provinces, and 70:30 in the western provinces.
- *Pearl River basin:* Four types of vessels were eligible for government subsidies: lockage vessels with less than 300 tons of gross tonnage in the Xijiang River trunk waterway, single-hull chemical tankers and single-hull oil tankers, vessels that needed to be reconstructed to prevent waste pollution, and old inland vessels. New-model vessels in the Pearl River basin that met relevant requirements also were eligible for subsidies. The Ministry of Transport did not issue separate economic incentive policies for barge standardization in the Pearl River basin; they were included in the general scheme developed during the 12th Five-Year Plan period (2011–15).

Results of barge standardization projects

The barge standardization program resulted in the massive upgrading of the Chinese inland vessel fleet. Outdated vessels were removed from the market and replaced by larger, more efficient, and cleaner vessels. The number of vessels decreased, but average vessel size substantially increased (figure 3.4). The result was a huge increase in carrying capacity, which now meets China's growing traffic demands of the new economy.

As a result of the fleet renewal, the average vessel is now relatively young. Panel a of figure 3.5 shows that the average age of a vessel is now between eight and 15 years, which is quite young compared with other countries, where IWT vessels remain in service for several decades.

Usually an older fleet means that the engines are old—older vessels produce more emissions than younger vessels. And, many of the newer vessels are larger than the older ones, as shown in panel b of figure 3.5.

The standardization of barges could only start after the waterways were classified because these two elements are closely related. The standardization of barges was seen as a precondition for fleet upgrading programs, and considering the size of the fleet (high share of small vessels) and the need for technical upgrading to improve safety, standardization was the only way to do this in a cost-efficient manner. The programs were open for large (public) shipping companies, but also for small (private) family vessel owners. The program gave

FIGURE 3.4

Size of China's inland vessel fleet, 1995–2018

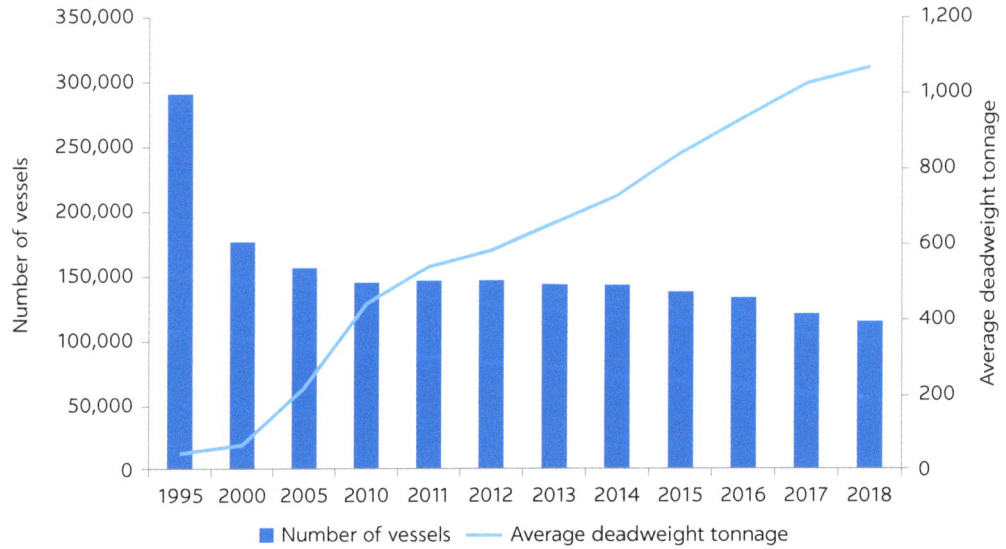

Source: China Waterborne Transport Research Institute data.

FIGURE 3.5

Average age of vessels in China by cargo type, 2017

a. By type of vessel and cargo

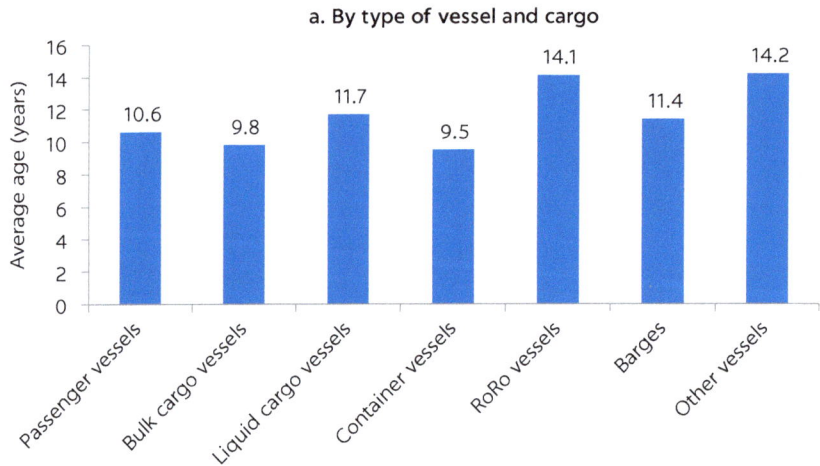

b. By size of vessel

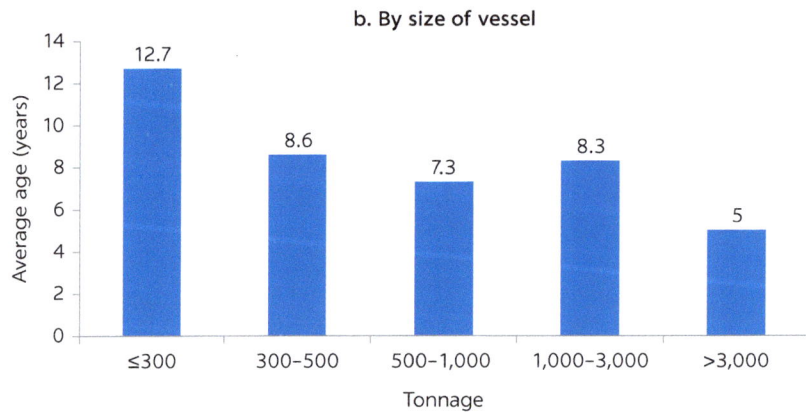

Source: China Waterborne Transport Research Institute data.
Note: RoRo = roll-on/roll-off.

technological support and financial compensation, but also it led to limitations for specific vessels on specific waterway sections. In addition, the program was used to stimulate the west and middle provinces because the split between central and provincial support was different (west: 70:30, middle: 60:40, and coastal/east: 50:50).

As a result, polluting vessels—such as single-hull chemical vessels, concrete barges, small tankers, and vessels without waste oil isolators—were slowly removed from the market. In 2018, around 30 percent of inland vessels still were not standardized; some shipowners chose to retrofit with standardized equipment rather than replacing the entire vessel.

EDUCATION AND TRAINING IN INLAND WATERWAY TRANSPORT

As the water transport market was reformed in the 1980s to meet transport demands, the Ministry of Transport opened the transport market to all parties (according to Minister Li Qing at a 1983 national transport conference, "the road opens to every vehicle, the water opens to every vessel"). As a result, more privately owned inland vessels entered the market. While publicly owned companies had larger vessels and systematic management, private ship owners lacked experience with inland vessel maneuvering and engine maintenance. The entry of private ship owners—along with the modernization of the IWT sector, the growth of international trade, and the adoption of new information and communication technologies—increased the need for logistics management and middle- and higher-level management staff in inland shipping companies. In addition, the modernization of the sector required ever-increasing skills by the staff and crew of inland shipping companies. Reforms in the educational system were needed to meet the growing demands.

China's universities and all levels of professional schools were quickly revived at the start of reform and the opening-up period to meet the demand for IWT personnel. For example, Chongqing, which is located upstream on the Yangtze about 2,200 kilometers from the coast, had at that time one university and six schools at different levels, all of which were certified to provide vessel maneuvering and engine room management. Wuhan, located along the middle of the Yangtze, had nine schools at all levels to provide relevant education.

The administrative system for the Dalian Maritime College, the Wuhan Maritime Engineering College, the Shanghai Maritime College, and the Nantong Medical College were reformed as part of the reform and opening up. They were then under the dual leadership of the Ministry of Transport and the authorities of the provinces and cities where the schools were located. The Ministry of Transport also restored the Chongqing Jiaotong College and strengthened the education capacity of secondary schools, including the Nanjing Marine Engineering Institute, the Wuhan Institute of Water Transportation, the Xiamen Jimei Navigation College, and the Nanjing River Transportation Secondary School.

As part of the reform process, the central government increased the autonomy of water transport education institutions and determined it would only offer guidance.

In November 1979, the Ministry of Transport held a meeting of the affiliated colleges. The focus was on adjustment, revision, and implementation of the "three fixed systems" (fixed profession, fixed scale, and fixed institutional size). Revision of the capital construction plan for schools during the three-year adjustment period was discussed, and issues concerning teaching, faculty strengthening, construction of laboratories, and development of teaching material were discussed and studied.

In 1983, to meet the transport industry's need for specialized personnel, the Ministry of Transport conducted a survey about the existing specialized personnel in transportation and forecasted demand for them, including in water transport. The ministry proposed that the focus should be on developing the basic backbone professions that are necessary for the development of water transport, such as ship handling, marine engineering management, marine communication and navigation, electrical management of ships, port and waterway engineering, and transportation management.

Following the survey, the ministry organized a seminar on maritime navigation education reform, at which training orientation, educational levels, and the educational structure of water transport education were discussed. Seminars on educational reforms in the following years focused on the knowledge level, size, and quality requirements of shipping companies. Governments, enterprises, and educational institutions discussed the reform of water transport education, with the goal of finding realistic and operational directions.

In 1990, the Ministry of Transport held a national conference on transportation education to comprehensively review and summarize the achievements, lessons learned, and shortcomings in transportation education since the reform and opening up and to discuss the guiding ideology and objectives of transportation education. At the conference, the need to "run schools on demand of transportation industry" to promote the sustained, stable, and coordinated development of education was noted.

In September 1990, the Ministry of Transport issued the "Outline of Regular Higher Education Planning in Transportation, the Outline of Vocational and Technical Planning in Transportation," and the "Outline of Adult Education Planning in Transportation during the Eighth Five-Year Plan Period," which together identified the guiding ideology, basic principles, development objectives, and main tasks for transportation education. In 1992, the ministry issued the "Notice on Deepening Reform and Expanding Autonomy in Regular Institutions of Higher Education," which enabled institutions of higher education in transportation to become more self-reliant in running such institutions, facilitated through reform policies.

To more actively adapt to the development needs of the water transport industry, the Ministry of Transport made changes to the original water transport educational institutions, and it established new institutions. In 1992, the Wuhan Maritime Engineering College merged with the Wuhan Institute of Water Transportation, officially changing its name to Wuhan Transportation University. The aim of the merger was to train more students for China's transportation industry, especially IWT and maritime transport. In 1994, the Dalian Maritime College changed its name to Dalian Maritime University. The establishment and development of the two universities created enabling conditions for improving the educational quality and academic level of navigation and water transport engineering in China.

BOX 3.6

Harmonized training and education in inland navigation within Europe's EDINNA network

The harmonization of training requirements and certification of crew members is an essential element in the development of an IWT system in which operators and crew work in different waterway areas. Harmonized training and education are critical to realizing the standards for safe and clean IWT operations.

With a common market established and the accession of new members with IWT systems, the European Union was confronted with different practices, standards, and qualification requirements for IWT. To address these issues, in June 2008 during a roundtable conference of the Central Commission for the Navigation on the Rhine in Strasbourg, directors and managers of the participating institutions signed a memorandum of understanding to create and formalize the Educational Network of Inland Waterway Navigation Schools and Training Institutes (EDINNA). Through EDINNA, the sector is working to harmonize training and education in IWT. It has developed sets of standardized training packages and courses to ensure that the staffs of vessels receive qualified training. In addition, to improve training and international cooperation, EDINNA has opened membership to all countries.

Source: https://www.edinna.eu/.

The Ministry of Transport and local governments have jointly set up several water transport vocational schools, including the Guangzhou Maritime Institute (established in 1992), the Maritime College of Jimei University (established in 1998), and the Water Transport Vocational and Technical College of Wuhan Transportation University (established in 1999).

At a national conference in 1995, experiences in transportation education reform and development were exchanged. The minister of transport proposed sharpening the focus on two areas: the construction of transportation infrastructure and the training of transportation personnel. Transportation leaders at all levels agreed on those priorities. Great efforts followed in education, science, and technology to implement the strategic decision of developing the country through science and education. In 2010, the Ministry of Transport formulated the "Ninth Five-Year Plan and the Development Plan for Transportation Education" on the basis of the recommendations of the State Education Commission.

China's system of inland shipping universities and schools is unique—it is the only country in the world that has inland shipping universities. Elsewhere in the world, inland shipping education normally is limited to vocational schools and training institutes (box 3.6).

STRENGTHENING RESEARCH AND DEVELOPMENT IN TRANSPORTATION SCIENCE AND TECHNOLOGY

The rapid development of China's IWT industry would not have been possible without major innovations in the sector that emerged from R&D programs. Waterways are different from railways and roads, in the sense that each river has its own characteristics and may require specific and dedicated solutions.

Technologies imported from other waterway basins may not be fully adaptable to local characteristics because of differences in geography, currents, climate, and even modes of economic development.

Projects like the Three Gorges Dam and locks and the deep-water channel at the Yangtze estuary area faced unique environments and challenges. No existing technologies were applicable; new and independent research was essential.

The Ministry of Transport set up several research centers to tackle the challenges of key IWT projects. The centers were active in upgrading technologies in IWT and adapting international standards and practices to local situations. Examples of their work included barge standardization programs, the implementation of ICT and river information services, and the greening of IWT. As a result of investments in R&D in IWT, China is now a leading innovator in several areas. Because of the scale of its market and fleet, it is in a strong position to develop and test new technologies, such as autonomous shipping and emission-free vessels.

As part of the reform process, many policies and actions have been initiated. In March 1978, the Central Committee of the Communist Party and the State Council held a national conference on science in Beijing. It was a milestone in the history of China's scientific and technological development and an important symbol of China's reform and opening up. The main message of the conference was that the "the key to modernization is the modernization of science and technology." The conference reversed the policy deviation and put scientific and technological work back on the right track. The same month, the Ministry of Transport convened a national conference on science and technology in the transportation system. It set out the tasks of developing transportation science and technology in the "Transport Science and Technology Development Plan for the Period of 1978–85" and put forward the goal of modernizing transport. Focusing on the reform of the operating mechanism and management system, the transportation research institutions have studied the commercialization of technological achievements, the development of the technology market, and the reform of the system for allocating funds. Reforms such as reducing allocations for operating expenses in science and technology, implementing management responsibility, developing internal contract systems, and transforming the system into enterprises gradually allowed the market mechanism to play a larger role in the operation of scientific research institutes. Substantial changes in the transportation science and technology system and its operation have promoted the integration of science and technology in traffic/transport construction and transportation. Most scientific research institutions in this field have adapted to economic development and gradually have become more self-reliant in directing research areas, in accordance with market mechanisms and national reform.

During the period of reform, several technical breakthroughs have been achieved in the construction of water transport infrastructure and the implementation of transport operations through dedicated investments in key research projects, development of technological equipment and installations, and industry participation. For example, in 1995, the Ministry of Transport invested ¥136 million (about US$20 million) in the Yangtze Estuary Deepwater Channel Science Experiment Center to ensure the smooth implementation of the Yangtze estuary deep-water channel regulation project. The objective of the center was to optimize and validate designs, guide construction, and provide the necessary basic research facilities to further study channel regulation and deepening. Established in conjunction with key state projects, the center played an important role in the construction and regulation of the Yangtze estuary deep-water channel.

In 2001, the Ministry of Transport convened the National Working Conference on Transport Science and Technology Innovation, at which new measures to promote scientific and technological innovation were proposed. The conference emphasized that enterprises are the main body for technological progress and innovation and that full use should be made of the facilities and students at universities and scientific research institutions. Conference attendees recommended strengthening the technological ability of enterprises by combining production, education, and research. The same year, China launched its western transportation construction science and technology project, to coordinate with the western development program. In 2005, the Ministry of Transport compiled the "Medium and Long-Term Science and Technology Development Planning Outline for Highway and Water Transportation (2006–20)." It clarified the guiding principles, development goals, key tasks, implementation schemes, and safeguard measures for highway and waterway transportation science and technology development.

IMPACT OF POLICY MEASURES AND REFORMS ON QUALITY AND PERFORMANCE OF INLAND WATERWAY TRANSPORT IN CHINA

For Chinese shipping companies, IWT represents a major share of their business. In 2018, IWT accounted for 53.3 percent of all waterborne transport by Chinese shipping companies (see figure 3.6), which was significantly more than coastal shipping and ocean freight. The growth of the IWT sector is linked to 16 specific policy measures that led to dramatic increases in cargo volumes (see figure 3.7).

As the 16 policies in figure 3.7 illustrate, the focus of IWT policy and reforms shifted from pure infrastructure-oriented policies to the development of

FIGURE 3.6

Waterborne transport in China by Chinese shipping companies, 2018

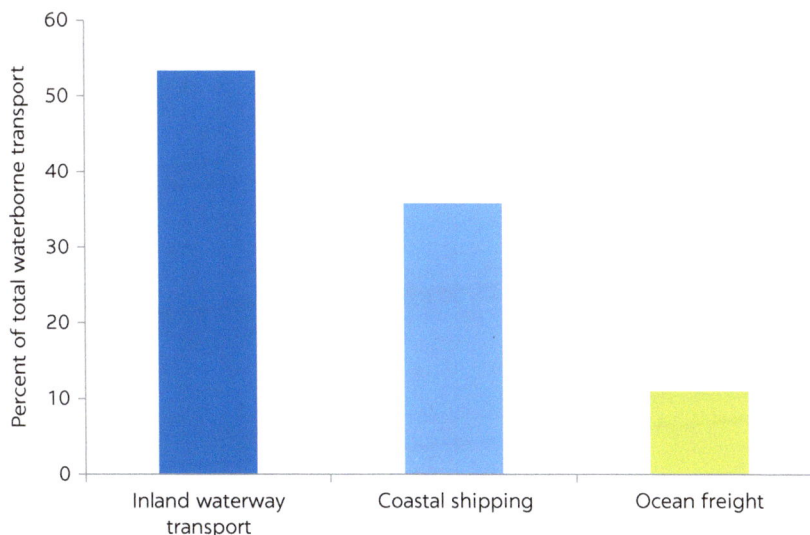

Source: China Waterborne Transport Research Institute data.

FIGURE 3.7

Cargo volumes on China's waterways and ports and timeline of policy reforms, 1978–2018

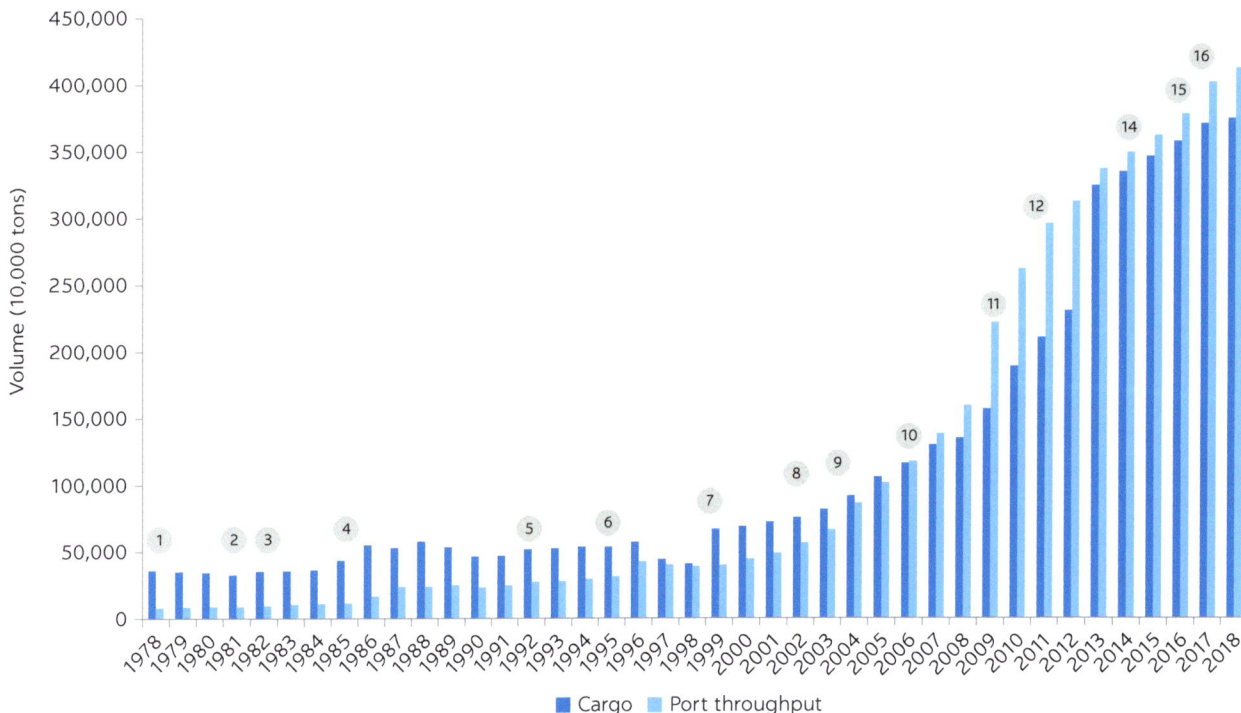

Source: China Waterborne Transport Research Institute data.

Note: 16 benchmark policies have catalyzed IWT in China:

① Instruction and the call for "changing the situation of ports in three years," results in the construction and expansion of several 10,000-ton terminals.

② Ministry of Transport sets up IWT administration to accelerate development of IWT.

③ The Ministry of Transport submits to State Council the reform plan for the Yangtze River shipping system, which was formally approved on March 25, 1983. The first step of the reform is to separate the management of ports from shipping and to separate the government function from enterprise management. The Ministry of Transport puts forward the guideline that "navigation is allowed for everyone and driving is allowed for everyone, connected trunks and branches, directed trunks and branches."

④ Trial collection of port construction fees begins with the aim of strengthening port construction. In February 1986, the State Standard Bureau promulgates two national standards: "Aids to Navigation on Inland Waterways" and "Main Dimensions of Aids to Navigation on Inland Waterways."

⑤ In August 1992, the Ministry of Transport, Ministry of Finance, and State Price Control Bureau jointly issue "Measures for the Collection and Use of Maintenance Fees for Inland Waterways," to further clarify the scope of the collection of waterway maintenance fees, to adjust the collection standard, to specify that waterway maintenance fees shall be collected and managed by waterway management organizations under the transportation departments at various levels, and to strengthen management of use of waterway maintenance fees.

⑥ National conference on IWT development is held. The minister of transport clarifies several issues, including the policies of "overall planning, combination of central and regional systems, responsibility distribution at different levels and joint construction"; of building the main water transport channel with "one vertical route and three horizontal routes"; and of constructing ports, wharfs, and supporting safeguard systems. With the approval of the State Council, the construction fund for IWT is established, with the purpose of constructing terminal infrastructure and regulating waterways by focusing on the construction of main hubs and main channels.

⑦ To promote the implementation of the western development strategy, the Ministry of Transport issues the "Outline of Inland Waterway Transport Development in Western China in 2000," which clarifies overall development objectives. They include the following: form the main water transport channel linking rivers and seas in the western region in 20 years; develop and construct main tributary waterways and port facilities and form a supporting service system for IWT; and, by the middle of the twenty-first century, realize a modern IWT system that has the main water transport channel as its backbone and includes the connection of trunk and branch waterways, the use of modern facilities and equipment, and coordinated high-quality land and water transport services.

⑧ On December 15, the Ministry of Transport—together with the governments of Shandong, Jiangsu, Zhejiang, Henan, Anhui, and Shanghai—issue the "Action Plan for Barge Standardization Demonstration Project of the Grand Canal."

⑨ During 2004–05, the Ministry of Transport issues the "Plan (Key Points) for High-Grade Waterway Networks" in the Yangtze River Delta and the Pearl River Delta. These plans, which set target years of 2010 and 2020, respectively, determine the core and backbone role of the high-grade waterway networks in the regional inland waterway system.

⑩ The State Council approves the implementation of the "Layout Plan of National Inland Waterways and Ports." Planned waterway upgrades cover about 19,000 kilometers, including 14,300 kilometers of Class III and above waterways and 4,800 kilometers of Class IV waterways.

⑪ To accelerate barge standardization for the Yangtze River trunk waterway, the Ministry of Transport and Ministry of Finance—together with the governments of Shanghai, Chongqing, and the provinces of Jiangsu, Anhui, Jiangxi, Hubei, Hunan, Sichuan, Yunnan, and Henan provinces—formulate and issue the "Implementation Plan for Promoting the Barge Standardization for the Yangtze River Trunk Waterway," which comes into force on October 1, 2009.

Source continued on next page

⑫ The State Council issues the "Guideline of the State Council on Speeding up the Development of Inland Waterway Transport Including the Yangtze River," indicating that the development of IWT has become a national strategy. The guideline is marked as the start of a new round of development and opening up of the market along the Yangtze River Economic Belt and the Xijiang River Economic Belt.
⑬ To implement the 12th Five-Year Plan (2011–15) and the "Guideline on Speeding up the Development of Inland Waterway Transport Including the Yangtze River" and to promote the national barge standardization, the Ministry of Transport formulates the "Implementation Plan for Promoting National Barge Standardization."
⑭ The State Council issues the "Guideline on Promoting the Development of the Yangtze River Economic Belt by Relying on the Golden Waterway," which cites the need to give full play to the advantages of the Yangtze River, such as the capacity, low cost, and low energy consumption of IWT; to accelerate the improvement of the trunk waterway system of the Yangtze River; to regulate and dredge the downstream waterways; to effectively ease the bottlenecks of the upper and middle reaches; to improve the navigation conditions of tributaries; to optimize the functional layout of ports; to strengthen the construction of a collecting and dispatching system; to develop combined river-sea transportation and direct transport between trunk and branch waterways; and, to create a smooth, efficient, safe, and green golden waterway.
⑮ On December 7, 2016, the National Development and Reform Commission issues the "Implementation Plan for the Construction of Multimodal Transport of Ports along the Yangtze River Economic Belt During the 13th Five-Year Plan" to implement the development strategy for the Yangtze River Economic Belt, to promote the integrated development of transportation and logistics, to accelerate the construction of the collecting and dispatching system of ports along the Yangtze River, and to improve cargo transshipment capacity and efficiency as well as transportation service quality,
⑯ On August 4, 2017, the Ministry of Transport issues the "Guideline on Promoting the Green Shipping Development of the Yangtze River Economic Belt."

supporting systems and the improvement of the quality and performance of the IWT system as a whole—a move from quantity to quality.

The many reforms and policy changes were not taken in a sequential and neat manner but rather through a series of trial-and-error stages. The existence of feedback loops in China's IWT policy illustrated the fact that institutional reform is not straightforward.

During the early years of reform, attention was focused on the development of the major waterways and the capacity increase of ports. Once the standardization of the waterways was realized, China took up the upgrading of the fleet (through the barge standardization program) and the development of supporting systems, such as information technology, incentives, and funding. With the trunk waterway system online, the development of tributaries started, along similar lines as those of the major waterways.

In recent years, greater attention has been given to improving environmental performance and preventing waste and spills. Elements of more recent policies include the integration of inland waterways in multimodal supply chains, improved multimodal connectivity, and improved planning of industrial and economic zones in combination with logistics zones and inland waterways.

Another milestone was the development of waterways in western China, which included the development of the middle and upstream sections of the Yangtze River and better water connectivity for these regions, which in turn provided a cheap and reliable transport system as the backbone for economic development. The construction of a series of dams and ship locks on the tributaries in the middle and upstream sections of the river increased the navigability of these waterways; the construction of the Three Gorges Dam, with its massive ship-lock system, opened the upstream section of the Yangtze River to larger vessels. The increase in capacity of the waterways contributed to substantially higher traffic in the upstream provinces. Because of these developments, the middle stream has increased its share of total throughput in the Yangtze ports (figure 3.8, panel a). And for container transport, the upstream section experienced the fastest growth (figure 3.8, panel b).

Total waterborne freight volumes reached 7 billion tons in 2018, accounting for 13.6 percent of total freight volume—a 5.4 percent increase in modal share over 1990 (figure 3.9, panel a). The volume of inland waterborne transport doubled in just eight years, between 2010 and 2018.

FIGURE 3.8

Throughput of downstream, middle-stream, and upstream ports in China, 1990–2018

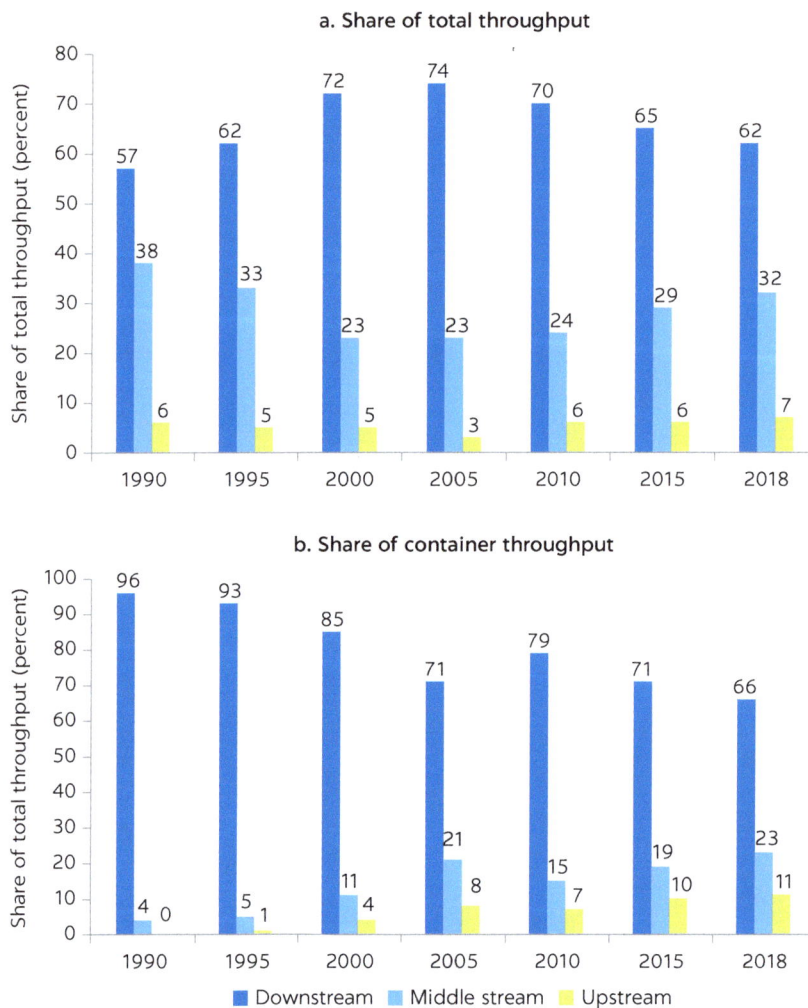

a. Share of total throughput

b. Share of container throughput

■ Downstream ■ Middle stream ■ Upstream

Source: China Waterborne Transport Research Institute data.

The freight performance of waterborne transport reached 9,905 billion ton-kilometers, 49.7 percent of the total freight transport performance (including road, rail, and air transport). This figure represented a 2 percent increase in modal share over 2013 and a 25.5 percent increase in absolute volume in the six years between 2013 and 2018 (figure 3.10, panel b).

Between 2000 and 2018, IWT's market share increased and shares of coastal and ocean transport declined in the water transport sector (figure 3.10). In 2018, inland waterway freight volume reached 3.74 billion tons, and its share of the total waterborne freight volume transported increased from nearly 50 percent (in 2010) to 53 percent. It should be noted that figure 3.10 only includes the volumes in ocean transport done by Chinese shipping companies. Chinese companies have an estimated share of 17 percent in total ocean transport to and from China.

These increases suggest that China's IWT policies have been successful in achieving important policy aims, including shifts to higher-value cargo, the development of the middle and upstream regions of the Yangtze, and larger IWT volumes and modal shares.

FIGURE 3.9

Modal share of transport volume and freight performance in China, 2013 and 2018

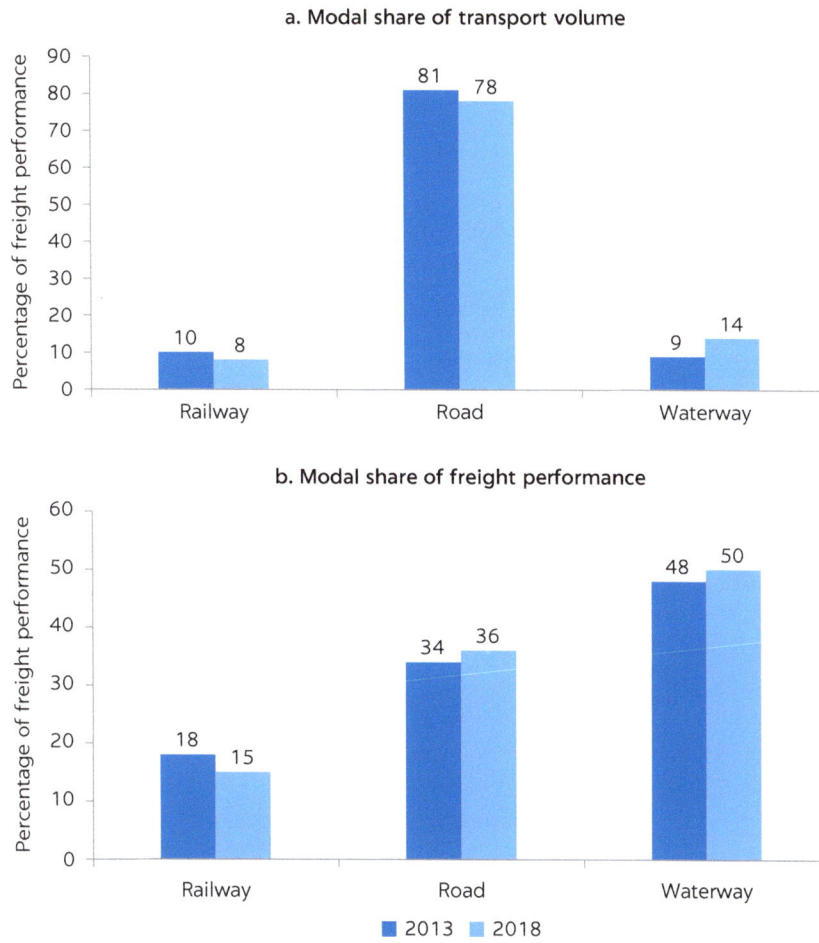

a. Modal share of transport volume

b. Modal share of freight performance

Source: China Waterborne Transport Research Institute data.

FIGURE 3.10

Inland waterway, coastal, and ocean transport freight volume in China by Chinese shipping companies, 2010 and 2018

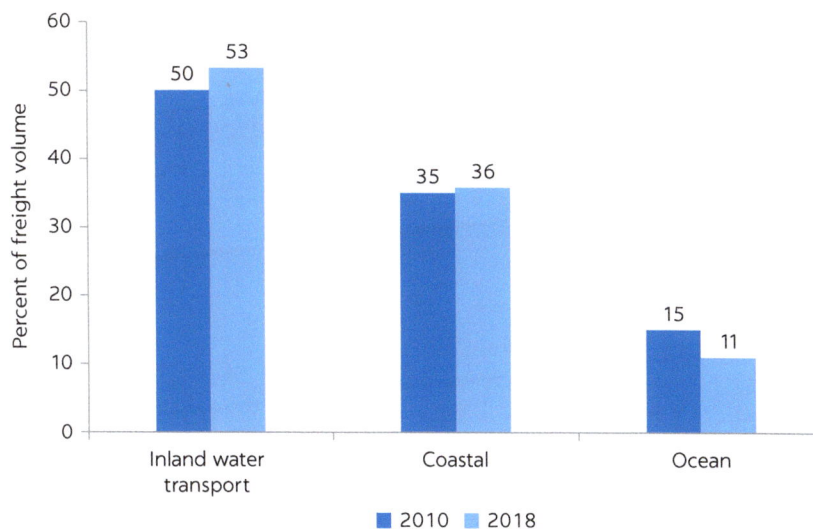

HIGHLIGHTS

- IWT development in China was guided by 16 key policy actions and programs that were focused on strengthening positive developments and adapting fewer positive developments.
- The many institutional reforms were not undertaken in a neat, sequential manner, but rather through a series of trial-and-error stages, with feedback loops used.
- Priorities and focus areas for IWT in China have changed in response to economic, environmental, and societal requirements.
- In the early years, much investment and attention were placed on hardware components. China invested in making fairways navigable and developing its ports. Subsequently, to accommodate larger vessels, waterways were deepened and made accessible by creating hydropower-cum-ship-lock complexes and classifying waterways.
- Classification of the waterways made it possible to develop standardized vessels. Several barge standardization schemes were set up to remove old and outdated vessels and to upgrade the fleet.
- The development of the IWT system facilitated the development of large industries along the waterways, transforming them into economic corridors. The development of middle and western China could not have been so successful without the vast IWT network.
- Recently, the focus has slowly shifted toward quality improvements, in addition to hardware development. Green solutions, management of hazardous cargo, waste, application of ICT and smart shipping, human resource management, and smart funding solutions have become focal points, with the aim of increasing efficiency, environmental performance, and safety.
- Much attention was given to the educational program and research and development, which resulted in a unique system of inland shipping universities and schools. Elsewhere in the world, inland shipping education usually is limited to vocational schools and training.
- An important lesson for other countries attempting to revive their IWT sectors is that China remained open to learning from other countries. Especially in the early years, IWT development drew heavily on international experiences and financing from international institutions, such as the World Bank, to introduce modern practices.

NOTE

1. The Changjiang National Shipping Company had managed trunk waterway ports, waterways, navigation administration, ships, public security, factories, scientific research, design, and educational and training institutions related to shipping. Its exclusive management contract gave it various governmental responsibilities and charged it with running several port and shipping enterprises.

REFERENCES

Chinese Policy Documents

Ministry of Finance, State Price Control Bureau, and Ministry of Transport. 1992. "Measures for the Collection and Use of Maintenance Fees for Inland Waterways."

Ministry of Transport. 1978a. "Outline of the Report on Modernization of Transportation."

——. 1978b. "Project Plan and Assignment Book of the Xijiang River Navigation Construction."

——. 1978c. "Transport Science and Technology Development Plan for the Period of 1978–1985."

——. 1983a. "Guideline Navigation Is Allowed for Everyone and Driving Is Allowed for Everyone, Connected Trunks and Branches, Directed Trunks and Branches."

——. 1983b. "Reform Plan for the Yangtze River Shipping System."

——. 1990a. "Outline of Adult Education Planning in Transportation during the 8th Five-Year Plan Period."

——. 1990b. "Outline of Regular Higher Education Planning in Transportation, Outline of Vocational and Technical Planning in Transportation."

——. 1992. "Notice on Deepening Reform and Expanding Autonomy in Regular Institutions of Higher Education."

——. 1994. "Work Outline for Technical Classification of Inland Waterways."

——. 1996. "Management Measures for Inland Waterway Navigation Aids."

——. 2000. "Outline of Inland Waterway Transport Development in Western China."

——. 2003. "Action Plan for Barge Standardization Demonstration Project of the Grand Canal."

——. 2004. "Plan (Key Points) for High-Class Waterway Network in the Yangtze River Delta."

——. 2005a. "Medium- and Long-Term Science and Technology Development Planning Outline for Highway and Water Transportation (2006–2020)."

——. 2005b. "Plan (Key Points) for High-Class Waterway Network in the Pearl River Delta."

——. 2006. "Outline of Development of Barge Standardization."

——. 2007. "Layout Plan of National Inland Waterways and Ports, National Development and Reform Committee."

——. 2010. "Ninth Five-Year Plan and the Development Plan for Transportation Education."

——. 2013. "Implementation Plan for Promoting National Barge Standardization during the 12th Five-Year Plan Period."

——. 2017. "Guideline on Promoting the Green Shipping Development of the Yangtze River Economic Belt."

Ministry of Transport and Ministry of Finance. 2009a. "Implementation Plan for Promoting the Barge Standardization for the Yangtze River Trunk Waterway."

——. 2009b. "Measures for the Management of Subsidy Funds for Barge Standardization for the Yangtze River Trunk Waterway."

Ministry of Transportation and provincial government of nine provinces and cities along the Yangtze. 2005. "Overall Plan for Promoting the Construction of the Yangtze River Golden Waterway during the 11th Five-Year Plan."

——. 2018. "Three-Year Action Plan for Structural Adjustment of Transportation from 2018 to 2020."

National Development and Reform Committee. 2016. "Implementation Plan for the Construction of Multimodal Transport of Ports along the Yangtze River Economic Belt during the 13th Five-Year Plan."

State Council. 1995. "Regulations of the People's Republic of China for Navigation Aids."

——. 2006. "Decision of the State Council on Strengthening Energy Conservation."

——. 2011. "Guideline on Speeding up the Development of Inland Waterway Transport Including the Yangtze River."

——. 2014. "Guideline on Promoting the Development of the Yangtze River Economic Belt by Relying on the Golden Waterway."

——. 2015. "Ten Measures for Air Pollution Prevention and Control, Action Plan for Water Pollution Prevention and Control, and Action Plan for Soil Pollution Prevention and Control."

State Standard Bureau. 1986. "Aids to Navigation on Inland Waterways."

——. 1986. "Main Dimensions of Aids to Navigation on Inland Waterways."

Other References

Beyer, Antoine. 2018. "Inland Waterways, Transport Corridors and Urban Waterfronts." International Transport Forum Discussion Paper 2018-21. Organisation for Economic Co-operation and Development, International Transport Forum, Paris. http://dx.doi .org/10.1787/c78b9c58-en.

——. 2008. *China's Transportation Opening Up and Reform 30 Years*. Beijing: China Communications Press Co., Ltd.

——. 2018. *China's Transportation Opening Up and Reform 40 Years*. Beijing: China Communications Press Co., Ltd.

European Commission. 2013. "NAIADES II: Towards Quality Inland Waterway Transport." Brussels.

Huijun, Gao. 2015. *Standardization for Inland Ships*. China Communications Press Co., Ltd.

4 Current Priorities for Inland Waterway Transport in China

China launched many inland waterway transport (IWT) programs and measures, sometimes through trial and error—pursuing successful paths and abandoning others. As a result of these programs, China's IWT infrastructure was greatly enhanced, the means for increasing the productivity of the sector was improved (that is, IWT terminals, equipment, and vessels), and the level of services, capacity, and availability was improved. China invested heavily in human resources and established vocational and educational programs to support IWT development. Progress was achieved through specific IWT policies that established the institutions and institutional framework, set rules and regulations, developed the planning mechanism, and funded activities.

These extraordinary achievements notwithstanding, there is still room for improvement. In several fields, Chinese research and development (R&D) in IWT is leading the way; this research could provide insights that benefit other waterway basins. However, China also could benefit from recent experiences and programs in other waterway basins. This chapter identifies current priorities and directions and describes several international practices and development directions from which China could potentially benefit. Some are already being adopted in China; others are being discussed.

IMPACT OF A CHANGING CHINA ON INLAND WATERWAY TRANSPORT

In 2013, China's economy entered a "new normal" state with a slowdown in economic growth (figure 4.1). Even with this slowdown, progress continues on structural adjustment, transformation, and upgrading to create a modern economic system.

More than half of economic growth is attributable to the services sector, and its share is still rising (figure 4.2). As a result of this structural change in the economy and rising private consumption, the composition of IWT cargo is slowly changing—as demand for containers grows and demand for coal, ore, minerals, construction materials, and other bulk commodities slows. For example, changing environmental policies have led to a growing demand for liquefied natural gas and for the development of roll-on/roll-off (RoRo) transport. New markets for IWT could develop because of the increase in biomass, urban distribution, e-commerce, and small shipments.

China's economic development has moved from the stage of high-speed growth to that of high-quality development. The main contradiction in society is now between people's growing desire for a better life and the unbalanced and

FIGURE 4.1

Annual GDP growth in China, 1978–2018

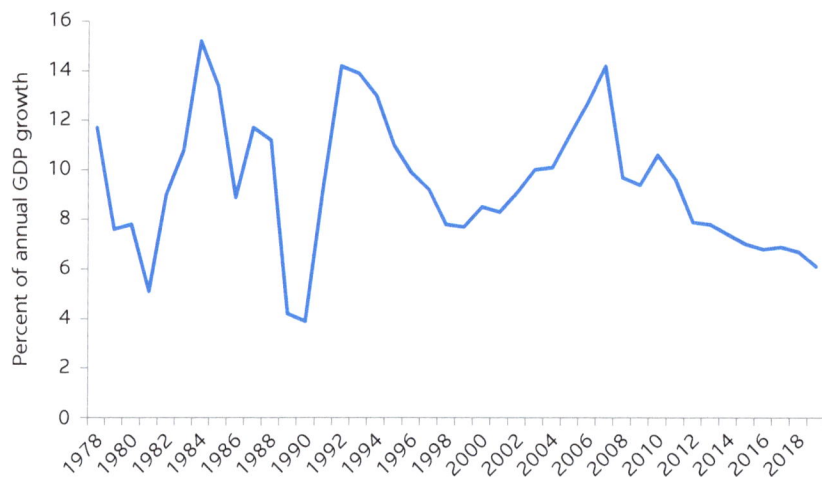

Source: China Waterborne Transport Research Institute data.

FIGURE 4.2

Sectoral composition of China's GDP, 1978–2018

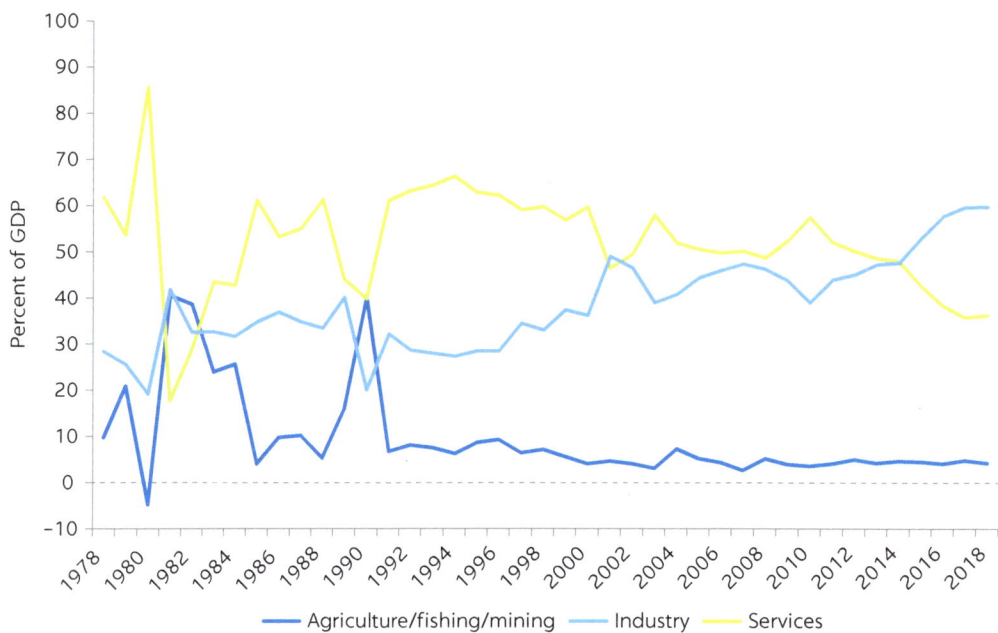

Source: China Waterborne Transport Research Institute data.

inadequate level of development. The new development concept of "innovation, coordination, green, open, and sharing" has an effect on all aspects of China's development, including the IWT sector.

The 2017 "Report of the 19th National Congress of the Communist Party of China" notes that China "should strive to build a moderately prosperous society in all aspects and embark on a new journey of building a modern socialist country in all aspects." It distinguishes several development stages (from 2020 to 2050) in realizing a strong modern socialist country that is prosperous, culturally advanced, harmonious, and beautiful because of modernization.

Retaining innovative development as a driving force

To keep up with the changing global context and state development goals, China needs to continue implementing its innovation-driven development strategy. Emphasis will be put on strengthening the role of science and technology as a driving force behind innovative development. For example, a recent initiative in the IWT sector is the establishment of a research center and test area for smart shipping, including autonomous sailing. China is one of only a few countries with a coordinated R&D program in this field. Big data, cloud computing, artificial intelligence, mobile internet, the Internet of Things, and other new technologies and business models have a profound effect on the development of the transport industry. Under their influence, IWT is moving in the direction of smart and high-efficiency development. Also, innovations in this field will contribute to a more efficient integration of IWT and other modes of transport.

Shared prosperity and narrowing regional differences

China has promoted the coordinated development of regions. To narrow regional gaps, it has increased its investment in fixed assets in the central and western regions to above the national average. Over the past 40 years, provincial differences in GDP per capita have narrowed and regional development has become more balanced (figure 4.3). The central and western regions have enjoyed above-average economic growth, as poverty alleviation efforts have deepened.

The Yangtze River Economic Belt serves as a coordinated development belt of interaction and cooperation among the eastern, central, and western regions. The waterway connection provides all regions access to all of the opportunities the coastal areas along the Yangtze River offer. The inland waterway sector plays a prominent role in regions where development of the service economy is relatively backward. The sector can contribute to coordinated development along the Yangtze River, the Pearl River, and other IWT regions.

Promoting green development

Economic and social development has improved the lives of the Chinese people— but it has also increased air pollution and caused environmental damage. To address the increase in pollution, the government of China issued several policy statements and initiatives such as "Ten Measures for Air Pollution Prevention and Control," "Action Plan for Water Pollution Prevention and Control," and

FIGURE 4.3

Difference in per capita GDP between richest and poorest provinces in China, 1978–2018

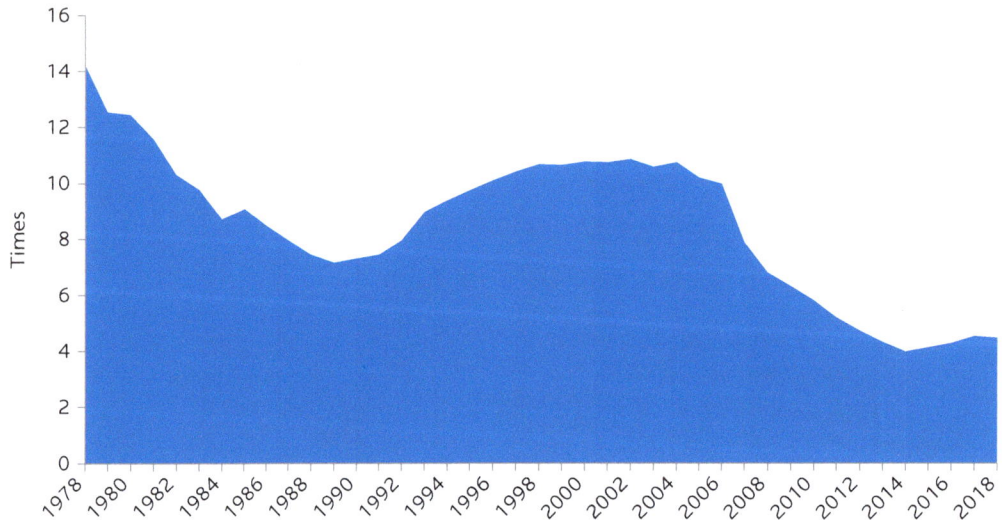

Source: China Waterborne Transport Research Institute data.

"Action Plan for Soil Pollution Prevention and Control" from 2013 to 2015. The overarching aim of these initiatives is for improvement in natural ecosystems and for ecological rehabilitation. As a result of the central government's policies, the concept of green development has become an important part of IWT development.

The comparative advantages of IWT have contributed to the development of a more integrated transport system combining transport modes. Larger IWT volumes and modal share reduce emission levels, energy use, and congestion relative to alternative transport systems, particularly road transport. Further greening remains a challenge and target for the IWT sector.

PRIORITIES FOR INLAND WATERWAY TRANSPORT IN CHINA

Making inland waterway transport greener

China has a large inland waterways vessel fleet—much larger than the fleets of Europe or the United States. Its impact on the environment of cities along the river, therefore, is substantial. The government has done much to reduce the negative impact of IWT on the environment—through its barge standardization projects (and associated increase in average vessel size that resulted from it); through the introduction of waste collection and emergency response systems; through the commissioning of studies and pilot projects on lower-emission vessels; and through incentive schemes for the mass implementation of new, clean technologies. However, more can and needs to be done.

The comparative advantages of IWT have increased as awareness of the importance of environmental protection has grown. China has been vigorously promoting the green development of IWT and must continue to do so. The Ministry of Transport has issued various plans for promoting green shipping on the inland waterway network including the following:[1]

- *Promoting the use of liquefied natural gas and other clean-energy vessels.* Pollution from vessels has a significant impact on the environment of cities along waterways. The Ministry of Transport has issued documents to promote the application of liquefied natural gas (LNG) vessels in IWT. The share of LNG vessels in the fleet must increase. And this increase in LNG vessels requires increasing the number of LNG filling stations and bunker vessels (see photo 4.1 for examples of the use of LNG in IWT). In addition to promoting the use of LNG, the government has promoted R&D on electric inland vessels.
- *Promoting the application of shore power.* The use of electric shore power in ship docking can reduce noise and air pollution. It is less harmful to the health of people onboard and to the people in the vicinity of ports than running diesel engines/generators. Also, because shore power is less expensive than diesel, using it reduces ships' operating costs. Some shore

PHOTO 4.1

Liquefied natural gas engines, vessels, and bunkering facilities

Source: © STC-NESTRA. Used with the permission of STC-NESTRA. Further permission required for reuse.
Note: Clockwise: Liquefied natural gas (LNG) vessels, LNG tank, LNG engine, LNG tank installed on a vessel, LNG bunkering station.

power facilities have already been built along the Yangtze River and the Pearl River.

- **Reducing ship garbage and oil sewage.** Many inland waterway ship owners live on ships with their families year-round, producing large volumes of household waste and sewage. The Yangtze River Administration of Navigational Affairs has established overwater tank-cleaning stations to reduce this pollution from ships. And it has established and improved tank-cleaning stations for chemical transportation (see photo 4.2).

- **Promoting ecologically friendly technologies and building ecological waterways.** During the construction of new ship locks, environmental protection assessments must be carried out following strict guidelines. For example, the construction of fish passes must be considered in the engineering design scheme. During construction, strict environmental protection and green construction are to be carried out to minimize the damage to the ecological environment. In areas with high levels of economic activity, compensation measures, such as the planting of reeds and trees, are adopted to improve the inland waterway environment. When possible, opportunities for shaping ecological corridors and developing water tourism will be explored.

- **Preventing illegal sand mining in inland rivers.** In 2015, to protect riverbed resources, the government took its first measures to limit illegal sand mining. In 2018, the government began cracking down on this activity. Current efforts are focusing on creating trading markets for sand and gravel and creating a long-term mechanism for the supply of mineral construction materials.

- **Fostering the development of green ports.** In 2013, the Ministry of Transport promulgated the Green Port rating standard, which evaluates a port on the basis of several indicators along the dimensions of concept, action, management, and effect. Eight terminals reached the four-star Green Port standard in 2016. The Longtan Container Terminal (Phase I), in Nanjing, was the only inland water port to meet this standard. In the coming years, the government will continue to spur the development of green ports, expanding its efforts to other inland ports.

PHOTO 4.2

Overwater waste collection

Source: © STC-NESTRA. Used with the permission of STC-NESTRA. Further permission required for reuse.

Similar to China, the European Union is addressing the greening of IWT. Box 4.1 describes the state of affairs and initiatives in this field in the European Union.

Developing multimodal transport

Since the integration of different modal entities in the Ministry of Transport, the development of comprehensive transportation has accelerated. The "Three-Year Action Plan for Structural Adjustment of Transportation from 2018 to 2020" concludes that the weak links in the development of inland multimodal transport need to be strengthened:

BOX 4.1

What is the European Union doing to green its inland waterway transport?

China and the European Union are frontrunners in efforts to green the IWT sector. Other countries are also setting up pilot projects in this field, but their efforts are relatively small and nascent.

A major concern in the European Union is the emission of nitrogen oxides (NO_x) and particulate matter (PM). The current emission limit for IWT engines dates from 2007. It allows NO_x emission levels for a new engine that are about 15 times higher than for a new truck; for PM the difference is a factor of 20. Because of the higher volumes transported over longer distances, the overall environmental balance per ton-kilometer is still lowest for IWT, making it the most efficient mode of transport. But improvements are necessary to improve the environmental performance of the sector—and the technologies exist to do so. In addition, policy makers are seeking to impose environmental requirements comparable to those in competing transport sectors.

The European Union is striving to put the ambition of the Paris Agreements into force through a comprehensive set of measures:

- The implementation of higher-emission standards for new engines
- Securing financial support for initiatives and innovative research to further reduce emissions by IWT
- Exploring the uptake of alternative fuels for IWT by providing regulatory, financial, technical, and infrastructural support

- Reviewing possibilities for charging for the use of infrastructure to internalize external costs in IWT
- Requiring the providing of shore-side electricity facilities at IWT ports
- Sharing good practices on integrated approaches to sustainable inland waterway management in compliance with other waterway functions, in particular where ecology is a major concern
- Supporting the development and use of waste collection systems in IWT
- Implementing the upgrading of main inland waterways to reach the standards of minimum inland waterways Class IV, to reduce carbon emissions

The new European Green Deal resets the European Commission's commitment to tackle climate and environmental-related challenges. With regard to emissions, a 90 percent reduction in transport emissions is needed by 2050 to achieve climate neutrality, and all transport modes, including inland shipping, will have to contribute to the reduction. Fossil-fuel subsidies should end. As a matter of priority, a substantial part of the 75 percent of inland freight carried today by road should shift onto rail and inland waterways. Some individual EU member states have taken the initiative to secure sector and governments' commitment and funding to promote clean inland and sea shipping.

Sources: Inland Navigation Europe 2019; Government of the Netherlands 2019.

- *Implementing demonstration projects and promoting the structural adjustment of transportation.* Recently, China has promoted the formation of rail-river transportation hubs at major ports along the Yangtze River trunk waterway. From 2016 to 2018, the Ministry of Transport and the National Development and Reform Commission carried out three batches of multimodal transport demonstration projects, including nine inland river port multimodal transport projects. Inland river port companies in Jiangsu, Anhui, Hubei, Hunan, Chongqing, Sichuan, and other provinces along the Yangtze River conducted multimodal projects of containers, RoRo, and steel and other goods. Demonstration projects of multimodal transport in the middle reaches of the Yangtze River aimed at realizing seamless connections between container terminals and railway lines and giving full play to the comprehensive collaborative advantages of IWT.

- *Developing river-sea transport by innovating vessels.* The Zhoushan River–Ocean Combined Transportation Service Center and the Shanghai International Shipping Center of the Yangtze River Economic Belt have cooperated with provinces and cities along the Yangtze River to develop river-ocean transport of bulk commodities such as ore and coal and of containers. This mode of transport has become common in the Yangtze River Delta. The "Guideline on Promoting the Development of River–Sea Transportation on Specific Routes" (Ministry of Transport 2018) promotes the construction of vessels for river-sea transport to the Shanghai Yangshan Port and the Ningbo Zhoushan Port. Such transport can improve efficiency because it avoids transshipment in a seaport. The Shanghai Port and the Ningbo Zhoushan Port have taken steps to speed the development of the terminal at the north side of Xiaoyangshan, which serves as a transshipment base of river-sea vessels. Studies are under way for developing river-sea container traffic—including the operation of 1,100 twenty-foot equivalent unit (TEU) vessels between Wuhan and Yangshan, 124 TEU container vessels between inland ports in the Yangtze Delta area and Yangshan, and container vessels between Chongqing and Yangshan—that meets the technical requirements of vessels passing through the Three Gorges complex. The government is also studying the use of river-sea bulk cargo ships of 5,000–20,000 deadweight tons (DWT) between the main ports in the middle and lower reaches of the Yangtze River and Zhoushan. And it is promoting R&D of river-sea containers and bulk vessels from the main ports in the northern Jiangsu section of the Grand Canal to Lianyungang Port to improve the efficiency of transport on the Yangtze River.

The World Bank's support is changing in line with the changing priorities, and it is taking a wider approach, as illustrated in box 4.2.

Optimizing port capacity

To improve the service level of ports in China, the following actions have been taken:

- *Taking action against the illegal use of inland coastline terminals.* In October 2015, the leading national group for promoting the development of the Yangtze River Economic Belt led an effort to clean up illegal terminals and illegal sand mining along the Yangtze River trunk waterway. By the end of

BOX 4.2

World Bank engagement in the new era

In the new era of IWT development in China, the World Bank continues to demonstrate innovation in its support of and approach to Chinese IWT projects. The World Bank has adopted an integrated, multimodal approach that accounts for the challenges of multiple users of waterways and the impact of climate change.

For example, the development objectives of the World Bank's Global Environment Facility (GEF) Efficient and Green Freight Transport Project for China are to improve institutional capacity to formulate and evaluate policies and strategies to promote green freight transport systems and to pilot innovative carbon emission. The project, implemented on a national level and in four pilot provinces, has a number of components that relate to IWT. The national technical assistance component includes (a) the development of policy and strategy for a low-carbon multimodal freight transportation system; (b) the development of national policies and guidelines for green urban freight distribution; and (c) the development of an abatement cost analytical tool for freight transport emission reduction. The subnational technical assistance and pilot components include the integrated development of the inland waterway of the Han River. The third component relates to capacity building, monitoring and evaluation, and project management.

A second innovative project that demonstrates an integrated approach with an IWT component is the World Bank's financing of the Three Gorges Modern Logistics Center Infrastructure Project in Yichang (figure B4.2.1). The port of Yichang is a major inland waterway port located at the boundary of the middle reach and upper reach of the Yangtze River, 1,728 kilometers from Shanghai. The project brings a balanced IWT infrastructure and technology investment to support Yichang's vision to develop the port of Yichang into a major multimodal hub along the Yangtze River. The port has a projected capacity of 60 million tons, 1 million twenty-foot equivalent unit (TEU), and 400,000 commercial vehicles. Key features of the project include the following:

- Logistics-led industrial transformation in Yichang, Hubei Province
- Marketing strategy and business plan for comprehensive IWT port and logistics center operations that focus on consolidating and empowering local small and medium businesses
- Application of cloud-based solutions and blockchain technologies to improve overall logistics efficiency while reducing costs, especially for multimodal freight transport

FIGURE B4.2.1

Artistic depiction of the Three Gorges Modern Logistics Center

Source: World Bank.

May 2018, 1,254 illegal terminals along the Yangtze River trunk waterway had been dismantled and "regreened," and 107 had been upgraded. In Hubei Province, more than 1,100 terminals of various types have been removed and 143 kilometers of shoreline cleared, ecologically restoring a large area.

- *Promoting the sharing of public resources.* Efforts have been made to explore the construction and sharing of public resources such as waterways and anchorages in Jiangsu and other provinces to improve the service level of ports. Jiangsu Province is a good example of the promotion of the construction and sharing of public IWT resources. It actively provides support to help the Ministry of Transport deepen the waterway downstream of Nanjing to 12.5 meter, allowing much larger oceangoing vessels to navigate the section of the Yangtze in Jiangsu. Jiangsu also invested heavily in its small river network, which is the main part of the Yangtze Delta network (one of the two networks in the 2-1-2-1 network). The province has dredged bottleneck sections of this network, which is more than 3,000 kilometers long; modified or rebuilt bridges with low clearance, to connect ports along the Yangtze with high-class waterway networks; improved port connectivity; and facilitated the inland shipping business substantially.

- *Promoting the integration of regional ports and improving the efficiency of the use of port shoreline resources.* Provincial port groups established in Jiangsu, Anhui, and Hubei provinces have begun establishing provincial port corporations. Integrated operation has been achieved at the Yangluo container terminal in Wuhan, and dispatching under overall planning has been realized for the container business in Jiangsu Province. In addition, efforts are being made to facilitate asset integration to further improve port development. To spur the development of higher-quality operations in the Yangtze River Delta, ports in the region will take the lead in promoting the networking of inland waterways and the integration of regional ports and further optimizing the functional layout of those ports. The Shanghai International Port (Group) Co., Ltd., and the Zhejiang Seaport Group will jointly develop the terminal on the north side of Xiaoyangshan. Their efforts will accelerate the formation of a coordinated development pattern with the linkage of trunk and branch inland waterways and the improved layout of short-sea and ocean-going shipping routes. Efforts have also been made to promote the combined river-sea transport of containers and bulk cargo.

Box 4.3 describes the Trans-European Network for Transport and the ways in which Europe integrated inland waterways into a multimodal transport network by turning inland ports into multimodal logistics nodes.

Enhancing human resources, capacity building, and training

By the end of 2018, 806,000 registered crew members served on inland vessels in China. Because of poor working conditions and insufficient room for career development in IWT, many people in shipping prefer to work in coastal shipping, ocean shipping, or other industries. The overall quality of crew members of inland vessels is poor, which adversely affects the safe operation of vessels. Inadequate inflows of qualified crew members pose a risk to the sustainable and healthy development of the IWT industry. Improving working conditions in IWT and renumerations are of great importance for the sustainability of the IWT system over the long term. Efforts will be made to explore how the vocational development of crew members of inland vessels can be made more attractive to foster the inflow and sustainable talent team development. Improvements in technology and equipment may reduce manning requirements, lead to better working conditions for crews, and lower the costs of ship operations. Such development would require changes in training and redefinitions of the competencies of crew members.

BOX 4.3

Development of inland waterway transport infrastructure in Europe

The European inland waterway network is shaped mainly by large river basins (the two largest rivers are the Rhine and the Danube) and connecting rivers and canals. Parts of those waterways have been adjusted to accommodate the growing sizes of barges during the past century. With basins interconnected, the need for standardization of waterway dimensions became apparent. In 1954, the transport ministers of the European countries adopted the Conférence Européenne des Ministres des Transports (CEMT) classification to align inland waterway dimensions. The development of transport infrastructure in Europe is primarily the task of national governments, which follow cycles of long-term integrated transport strategies and project delivery. In many countries, the planning of inland waterways is assigned to executive agencies, such as the public works agency or the waterway agency.

Developing the Trans-European Network for Transport

The European Union has agreed on a policy of developing the Trans-European Network for Transport (TEN-T) and has created co-funding instruments for its realization. The objective of TEN-T policy is to contribute to a more efficient, sustainable, and safe transport system by developing a Europe-wide network of roads, railway lines, inland waterways, maritime shipping routes, ports, airports, and rail–road terminals. In 2013, it was agreed that there was a need for better streamlining and facilitating the coordinated development of the TEN-T core network, which was clustered into nine corridors. These corridors typically have multimodal infrastructures. Each corridor has a corridor management entity that, in close cooperation with stakeholders (national governments), defines an extensive list of priority investments. Financing schemes have been developed that work as multipliers. For example, the European Union (or the implementing European Investment Bank) guarantees certain investment loans extended by private banks.

Integrating inland waterways into a multimodal transport network

The first challenge is integrating inland waterways into a multimodal transport network, by turning inland ports into multimodal logistics nodes. An increasing share of IWT is part of a multimodal transport chain. Traditionally, IWT provided port-to-port transport of mainly commodities carried in bulk (coal, iron ore, sand and stones, oil, grain) that were stored or processed at the port. To be part of multimodal chains, inland ports must serve as comprehensive interfaces between waterborne and land transport modes (rail and road) and function as platforms of logistics services in their region. Local land use policies and infrastructure planning are enablers of this development, which benefits ports and IWT operators, increases transport efficiency, and reduces the negative external impacts of transport by bundling services and increasing the use of IWT. A few multimodal ports develop into multimodal hubs, which serve as connecting nodes between long-distance transport modes.

IWT in Europe developed from a stand-alone transport mode to a mode integrated in supply chains and multimodal transport networks. The inland port, often part of a larger logistic zone, has become one of the key elements in planning and developing the IWT network, as shown in figure B4.3.1.

The functionality of the inland port is changing, as illustrated in figure B4.3.2. Initially, inland ports were just transshipment points (I). Their function was then extended with logistic activities (II) and additional value-added services and light manufacturing and retailing (III).

Making waterway infrastructure smarter

The second challenge is making waterway infrastructure smarter. Doing so requires strengthening river information services (RIS), which aim to support safe and efficient navigation. Early RIS projects concerned standards for data and the exchange of information between users of the waterway and the waterway infrastructure manager. Progress has been made on

continued

Box 4.3, *continued*

the provision of electronic charts, electronic notices to skippers, and standards for electronic ship reporting. Public funding was used to create the information architecture; infrastructure and barge operators made mandatory investments in automatic identification system equipment.

The pace of implementation of RIS has varied. Projects are ongoing in different basins. Second-stage projects now focus more on corridor management, with information services shared by infrastructure and port authorities, waterway users, and related logistic partners. Corridor management focuses on a combination of port, cargo, vessels, and people, rather than on individually managed transport systems, modes, and nodes.

FIGURE B4.3.1

Integrated water terminal and logistics zone in Berlin

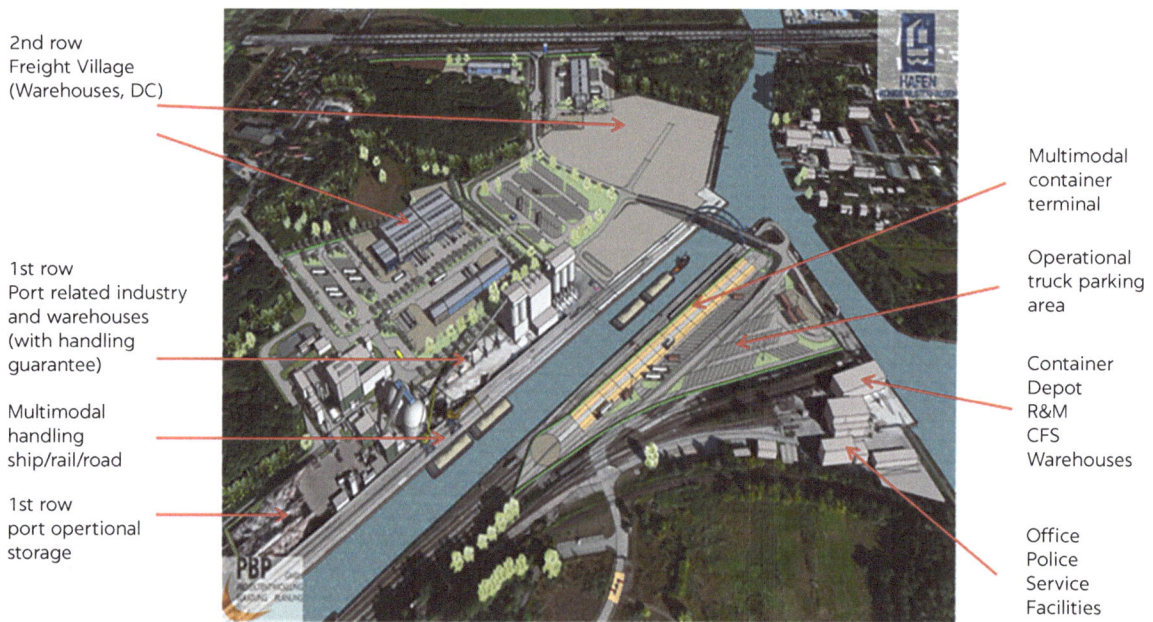

Source: LUTRA GmbH internal plan, edited by Wagener & Herbst.

FIGURE B4.3.2

Functionality of the modern inland port

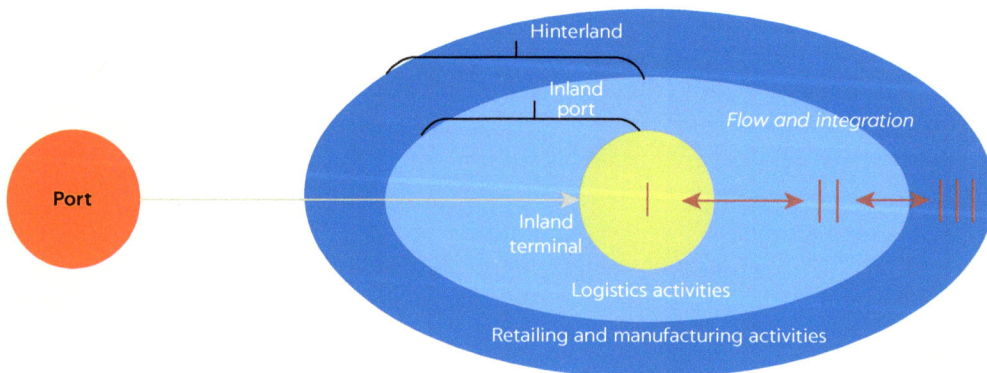

Source: STC-NESTRA data.

Regulating and enhancing standards

Regulating technical standards, staff qualifications, and working conditions helps maintain a high level of safety. Every waterway basin has its own sets of regulations for access to the market and profession and for operations and inspections. Vessel requirements relate to certification and regular inspections; crew requirements refer to professional qualifications of operating staff, such as staffing, working, and resting time on vessels. Technical standards also relate to vessel management, communication, and navigation charts, such as the set of rules for river information services (RIS). Some of the standards are country or water basin specific, some are applicable to wider areas, and some apply globally. Box 4.4 describes regulation outside of China.

BOX 4.4

Regulation of technical standards and qualifications in other countries

The European Union has issued a series of directives on technical requirements to enable vessels to navigate in all basins without barriers. Regulation ensures that there is a level playing field for vessel operators and it prevents price competition from leading to substandard transport services. Staffing regulations govern crew size and composition.

The existence of common directives makes it easier to update standards. The need for such updates has become evident, as major technological changes take place in navigation, port handling, management, and administration. Standards cover everything from automatic identification systems and navigation support to engine operations and electronic data exchanges.

Harmonization is especially important in crew qualifications. Associations of employers and employees are working together to reassess needs and propose regulation that will better fit those needs. These staffing innovations are taking place at a time when labor costs comprise a large share of vessel operation costs and it has become increasingly difficult to attract workers to the industry.

Crew regulations differ substantially across countries, especially for manning requirements. The technical state of the fleet, combined with labor costs, are the reasons for these differences. Education systems are needed that can adapt to increasing knowledge requirements (on the use of information and communication technology, the handling of hazardous substances, vessel technology, new engines, new fueling, and so forth). Better international cooperation is desirable. China's vessel standardization program is a good example of what standardization and harmonization can mean for vessel and fleet upgrading and improvements. It provides a valuable lesson for countries with similar needs.

India has followed a different path. The Inland Waterways Authority of India (IWAI) has developed sets of new (optimized) designs for specific waterways and specific vessel types, which it has made available for free on its website. Vessel owners and shipyards that are not able to design and test their own new vessels can work with these designs, which incentivize the standardization of new vessels.

River basins are increasingly interacting with one another, as good practices are shared. A good example is river information services, which have been adopted in water basins in the European Union, the United States, South America, and Asia, each with its own specifics. Adoption of good practices used elsewhere is seriously hampered by the fact that there is no institutionalized mechanism for exchange of knowledge in different areas. Information is dispersed, not published or published only in the original language, or limited to one specific area (such as infrastructure planning).

Promoting the innovative development of inland waterways

China has made progress in digitizing its IWT system, using data to improve efficiency and interaction among stakeholders:

- *Creating new business forms on the basis of the new generation of information technology.* E-commerce is developing rapidly in China, and new technologies and new business forms—big data, the Internet of Things, blockchain—are accelerating its penetration into traditional industries. The inland shipping market is actively trying to apply information and communication technology (ICT) to improve efficiency, reduce costs, and innovate business models. Many logistics platforms have been formed. They include Golden Horse Navigation cloud-based e-commerce, Wurunchuanlian, Changjianghui, and others. Companies like these match cargoes and ships, facilitate the joint procurement of spare parts and fuel oil, and provide financial services. The large number of small players in the Yangtze River shipping market makes it particularly suitable for e-commerce. For example, the Jiangsu Wurun United Shipping Internet Co., Ltd., can issue invoices and install video monitoring systems for registered ships, enabling shippers to monitor in real time whether their goods are properly managed. The reduction in cargo damage improves the customer experience and thus leads to higher freight charges, benefiting both shippers and shipowners, and helps increase the business scale. The Jiangsu Wurun United Shipping Internet Co., Ltd., also works with financial institutions, providing them with credit data on potential borrowers. On the basis of real-time transaction data, banks grant credit to small shipping companies.

- *Using information-based dispatching to increase efficiency.* Some busy waterway sections have introduced ship-lock management systems, using online vessel and voyage data. There are 11 ship locks along the northern Jiangsu section of the Grand Canal, with annual ship traffic volume exceeding 300 million tons. Ship density is extremely high. The Grand Canal Authority has created an information-based dispatching system, and it has developed a supporting mobile app to efficiently manage the passage of ships. Shipowners can make reservations and learn about current traffic conditions and waiting times. The Yangtze River basin has popularized the full-channel electronic navigational map. Intelligent scheduling systems are used in areas with busy ship traffic flow. Annual traffic volume of the Three Gorges ship lock exceeds 130 million tons; the optimal dispatch of ships is realized through an intelligent navigation management system that allows ships to safely pass through in the shortest time. Shanghai Port has built a navigation and logistics platform that has integrated several inland port enterprises owned by the Shanghai International Port Group (SIPG). The platform has functions for shipping schedule inquiries, container cargo inquiries, verified gross mass weighing, customs clearance information, and packing list pre-entry. It allows full tracking and querying of status.

  In 2017, the Ministry of Transport issued a list of 13 smart port demonstration projects. The key to smart ports is building a fully connected wireless network, realizing comprehensive awareness of port operation elements, and implementing automatic scheduling. An automated port control center and operators can perform operations such as video security monitoring and real-time data collection by using mobile terminals. These operations require a reliable low-latency network with real-time access to cloud data and a system with high security protection.

- *Using information to improve supervision and rescue.* The Digital Yangtze River project, which started in 2010, focuses on improving the search and rescue system on the Yangtze River trunk waterway. The supervision and monitoring of navigation and emergency response have been integrated in China for better searching and rescuing. China has also created a modern water supervision system in which GPS of key ships, closed circuit television of key waters, a vessel traffic service of key ports, and modern coastal patrol vessels complement one another. And, the digital transmission system project for data sharing and communication from Chongqing to Shanghai has been completed.

The European Union has made significant progress in digitizing its IWT system, using data to improve efficiency and interaction among stakeholders (box 4.5).

BOX 4.5

European efforts to make waterway infrastructure more efficient

The European Union is focusing on making waterway infrastructure smarter and providing additional services that make operations more efficient. The information available through river information services (RIS) can be used for much more than just managing vessel traffic and ensuring safety. Projects are under way that focus on corridor management. The RIS COMEX project, for example, is a multibeneficiary project that seeks to define, specify, implement, and sustainably operate corridor RIS services through the sharing of information by infrastructure managers, port authorities, waterway users, and logistic partners.

The Digital Inland Waterway Area (DINA) project interconnects information on infrastructure, people, operations, fleets, and cargo in the IWT sector and connects this information with other transport modes. The architecture that allows for the controlled sharing of this information can serve as a platform for future developments. DINA builds on existing investments and developments, such as components of the RIS. Proposed extensions would enable real-time data exchange and improved integration of other actors, such as shippers, logistics service providers, and inland ports. A planned data platform for barge operators will allow them to control data about their vessel, voyages, cargo, and crew. Barge operators will be able to use this information for their own purposes, including smart navigation, and also share it with other actors (for reporting purposes, for example). A new onboard toolkit (e-IWT) will probably be needed to connect barges with this digital environment and provide functionality for skippers, among other end users (European Commission and Directorate-General for Mobility and Transport 2017).

HIGHLIGHTS

- China's economy entered the "new normal" state in 2013, with a slowdown in economic growth. This slowdown had an effect on the IWT sector, and it changed some of the priorities.
- Now more than before, IWT's role is related to its contribution to society; IWT's role includes balancing economic developments between the regions, and supporting the efficient use of resources.
- Greening of IWT is a key priority and green initiatives indicate that there is still much to be gained in this field.
- Streamlining the unlimited growth of terminals and ports, and stimulating regional cooperation aims at an efficient use of shorelines.
- Improved multimodal connectivity and creation of economic zones along the waterways and close to ports supports the efficient use of waterways and the creation of multimodal logistics corridors.
- IWT development directions are supported by strong research and development and innovation programs.

NOTE

1. See the following documents: "Implementation Plan for Promoting Ecological Civilization Construction in Transportation" (Ministry of Transport 2017a); "Special Action Plan for Prevention and Control of Pollution from Ships in the Yangtze River Economic Belt (2018–20)" (Ministry of Transport 2017b); "Layout Plan of Anchorage for Dangerous Chemical Ships of the Yangtze River Trunk Waterway (2016–30)" (Ministry of Transport 2017c); "Layout Plan of Liquefied Natural Gas Filling Terminals along the Yangtze River Trunk Waterway, the Grand Canal, and the Xijiang River Trunk Waterway (2017–25)" (Ministry of Transport 2017d); "Layout Plan of Shore Power for Ports" (Ministry of Transport 2017e); "Guideline on Strengthening Supply Guarantee and Joint Supervision for Marine Low-Sulfur Fuel" (Ministry of Transport 2017f); and "Guideline on Promoting the Green Shipping Development of the Yangtze River Economic Belt" (Ministry of Transport 2017g).

REFERENCES

Chinese Policy Documents

Communist Party of China. 2017. "Report of the 19th National Congress of the Communist Party of China."

Ministry of Transport. 2017a. "Implementation Plan for Promoting Ecological Civilization Construction in Transportation."

——.2017b. "Special Action Plan for Prevention and Control of Pollution from Ships in the Yangtze River Economic Belt (2018–20)."

——. 2017c. "Layout Plan of Anchorage for Dangerous Chemical Ships of the Yangtze River Trunk Waterway (2016–30)."

——.2017d. "Layout Plan of Liquefied Natural Gas Filling Terminals along the Yangtze River Trunk Waterway, the Grand Canal and the Xijiang River Trunk Waterway (2017–25)."

——.2017e. "Layout Plan of Shore Power for Ports."

——.2017f. "Guideline on Strengthening Supply Guarantee and Joint Supervision for Marine Low-Sulfur Fuel."

——. 2017g. "Guideline on Promoting the Green Shipping Development of the Yangtze River Economic Belt."

——. 2018. "Guideline on Promoting the Development of River-Sea Transportation on Specific Routes."

Ministry of Transport and provincial government of nine provinces and cities along the Yangtze. 2018. "Three-Year Action Plan for Structural Adjustment of Transportation from 2018 to 2020."

State Council. 2015. "Ten Measures for Air Pollution Prevention and Control, Action Plan for Water Pollution Prevention and Control and Action Plan for Soil Pollution Prevention and Control."

Other References

European Commission and Directorate-General for Mobility and Transport. 2017. "Digital Inland Waterway Area: Towards a Digital Inland Waterway Area and Digital Multimodal Nodes."

Government of the Netherlands. 2019. "Sector and Governments Joining Forces to Promote Clean Inland and Sea Shipping." https://www.government.nl/latest/news/2019/06/14/sector-and-governments-joining-forces-to-promote-clean-inland-and-sea-shipping.

Inland Navigation Europe. 2019. "The EU Green Deal and Inland Waterways Transport." http://www.inlandnavigation.eu/news/policy/the-eu-green-deal-and-inland-waterways-transport.

5 Future Priorities for Inland Waterway Transport in China

INTRODUCTION

Several challenges need to be addressed in the coming years to keep inland waterway transport (IWT) competitive, to improve environmental performance, and to make full use of new technologies. Options for further reform and development directions are grouped in the following six areas:

- Markets, market development, and modal share
- Integrated water management, planning, and governance
- Greening and climate change adaptability
- Technological innovations and standardization
- Multimodal connectivity
- Smart inland shipping

MARKETS, MARKET DEVELOPMENT, AND MODAL SHARE

Expanding beyond areas near waterways

IWT in China is used mainly in areas close to waterways. Experience in other countries reveals that IWT can be an economically feasible solution in a much wider catchment area, once multimodal solutions are available. Shippers outside of the river environment are often not even aware of the possibilities of integrating IWT in their supply chains.

Despite recent developments, IWT in China still has a large share of low-value bulk goods. In contrast, in waterway basins in other countries, inland water vessels transport different types of goods and shipments, including small shipments, e-commerce, urban logistics, and short-distance transport, often as part of multimodal solutions. China's automobile manufacturers are concentrated in the Yangtze River and Pearl River regions, providing good conditions for the development of roll-on/roll-off (RoRo) vessels (photo 5.1). RoRo transport provides opportunities to develop various solutions that allow drivers to accompany the truck on the vessel, and other solutions, such as the pull and

PHOTO 5.1
Examples of roll-on/roll-off transport

Source: © STC-NESTRA. Used with the permission of STC-NESTRA. Further permission required for reuse.
Note: The image on the left shows truck RoRo transport. The image on the right shows passenger car RoRo transport.

hook system, in which only the trailer is transported on the vessel, without the truck and driver. RoRo is already used in the Three Gorges reservoir; it could be applied more widely. The construction of swap trailer yards and stations along the Yangtze River and Pearl River will be intensified. Industry standards for swap trailer transport need to be standardized, and regulatory procedures for industry development need to be optimized.

Creating an institutionalized system for observing the market

China does not have an institutionalized system for market observation, for the identification of new and potential markets, or for the promotion of IWT (other than subsidies for new vessels and demonstration projects). The development of a market observation tool would guide future developments and investments in the IWT sector.

Market observation targets the regular provision of data to identify general and structural trends within a sector, estimate economic performance, and draw up medium-term forecasts on the basis of econometric models. Such a tool is created on the basis of indicators of various aspects and factors affecting the market. The main approaches for the IWT sector capture the following factors:

- General and structural trends of supply and demand in the transport sector (carriage of goods and passengers)
- Market operating conditions (freight, cargo operating rate, operating costs, investment capacity, hydraulicity)
- Trends in the modal share of inland shipping in various markets
- Job market trends in connection with inland shipping
- Structure of the profession
- Safety

Europe established a market observation system several decades ago (box 5.1).

BOX 5.1

Use of market observation tools in the European Union

The European Union market observation tool developed from one that included only basic information on fleets and cargo to one that provides a complete picture of the IWT market, including general and structural trends within the inland shipping sector, economic performance, and medium-term forecasts. It is organized by the Central Commission for Navigation of the Rhine (CCNR). CCNR works with professional organizations, associations, and a group of experts in the profession to collect data. The system provides quarterly insights as well as publications on specific areas and markets.

Establishing a promotion office

China does not have an IWT promotion office. In other countries, promotion offices are sources of information for the logistics industry and its institutional environment that provide information about IWT's advantages, potential role, and innovations. Such offices can identify new and potential markets for IWT and set up discussions with cargo owners about the possibility of using IWT as part of their supply chains.

Shipping exchange centers were set up along the Yangtze River in Shanghai, Chongqing, Wuhan, and Nanjing. They can play important roles in a market observation system and in the promotion of IWT if their functionality is expanded.

The Chongqing Shipping Exchange was the first inland exchange in China. It provides information about ship transactions, loan guarantee programs for new vessels, job openings, vessel financing support, joint procurement of fuel and spare parts of ships, and freight rates on typical routes.

Promoting modal shift and attracting small and medium enterprises

Innovations in the IWT sector and the trend toward multimodal transport involve larger shipping and transport companies. Participation by small and medium enterprises (SMEs) is limited because entry barriers in the IWT sector are much higher than in the truck sector (investments are both larger and more complex). SMEs already in the sector—including family businesses on smaller waterways—face difficulties keeping up with innovation, automation, information and communication technology, and training and education. Promoting modal shift remains a necessity for all enterprises, but SMEs require special attention. Box 5.2 provides examples of how the European Union promoted a modal shift toward inland waterway transport.

BOX 5.2

The European Union's modal shift toward inland waterway transport

Even in mature IWT markets—such as China, Europe, and the United States—the IWT sector needs promotion, stimulation, awareness raising, and sometimes initial support for new services. Support mechanisms are an indispensable element of IWT development plans.

The European Union requires that governments not intervene in markets and not favor operators in particular transport modes. Within this constraint, the European Union and its member states promote and support IWT through various means, including the Navigation and Inland Waterway Action and Development in Europe (NAIADES) Action Program, which covers the following:

- *Promotion offices.* A number of EU countries have promotion offices for IWT and short sea shipping (coastal transport). Some promotion offices have been in operation for more than 25 years. Most are funded by the private sector, with support in some cases from national governments and international bodies. The offices provide information for the logistics industry on advantages, potential role, and innovations in the IWT sector, and they implement and manage improvement and promotion projects.
- *The Marco Polo Program.* Established in 2003, the Marco Polo Program sought to stimulate intermodal business development on new routes by providing financial support. In its early years, it granted subsidies per ton-kilometer of cargo shifted from the road to intermodal transport modes. Later, the subsidies covered start-up losses in the first years of operation of new services for cases where investment costs were high

and utilization rates of services (and, therefore, revenues) still needed to increase to break-even levels. These subsidies helped mitigate business development risk. The program ended in 2013, when its added value declined in a saturated market. During its 10 years of operation, it contributed to many new intermodal services by rail and water.
- *Cargo matchmaking.* The European Union sponsors regular events, organized by promotion offices, to bring together supply and demand and stimulate the use of IWT. Potential users and operators of IWT meet at regional events with names like "barge-to-business" and "river dating" to match supply and demand. These mechanisms have been effective in promoting IWT. Several countries have logistics adviser networks for IWT. Logistics specialists at the national or regional levels at IWT promotion centers or waterway organizations carry out cargo searches, approach shippers and traders, and analyze logistics chains with the aim of preparing consolidated business cases for IWT use.

There has been much debate about pricing instruments. Their introduction is highly controversial in the European Union because of the need to maintain mode neutrality. Many of the external costs of transport—congestion, air pollution, carbon emissions, noise, accidents—are not included in prices. Some policy makers favor policies that internalize those costs by imposing levies on transport operations. However, the EU regulatory framework allows levies only on the costs of operations and the maintenance of infrastructure.

Source: Analysis of various European promoting programs by STC-NESTRA.

INTEGRATED WATER MANAGEMENT, PLANNING, AND GOVERNANCE

The current water management system suffers from both overlaps and omissions. Some maritime systems are directly under the control of the central government; however, local maritime systems for inland waterway management also exist. Both the China Classification Society and the ship inspection bureau have the right to inspect ships. The standards of local administrative departments are generally low, and law enforcement standards are not uniform within a basin. Efforts must be made to gradually unify industry standards. Clarifying and adjusting technical standards for ship safety would help optimize the development environment for IWT. The certification requirements for passenger ships, crude-oil tankers, oil tankers, and carriers of liquefied natural gas and liquefied petroleum gas that affect public safety must be adjusted.

Establishing a basin-wide management organization

The Yangtze River and the Pearl River are managed by the Yangtze Waterway Bureau and the Pearl River Waterway Bureau, respectively. Because of growing volumes on the main waterways, better harmonization is needed and attention must be given to management of the waterway basin that aims for better coordination between stakeholders. For this harmonization, the following steps are necessary:

- Establish a basin-wide management organization.
- Strengthen coordination with the water conservancy department and municipal departments to establish the final plan for waterway development.
- Reduce restrictions on IWT development caused by bridges, tunnels, cables, pipelines, canals, buildings, and other structures.
- Increase the use of water resources.

Improving supervision at ports

The government continues to push forward the reform of "streamlining administration and delegating power, strengthening supervision, and optimizing services"; of accelerating information sharing by the maritime, waterway, and ship-lock administrative departments; and of exploring a comprehensive and unified supervision mode in areas where conditions permit. The goal of these reforms is to improve the level of supervision at ports. Further study of the reform of an integrated supervision system is needed for some river basins, such as the tributaries of the Yangtze River.

Protecting shoreline resources

Shoreline resources are nonrenewable and precious. To protect them, a plan for shoreline use in inland river areas needs to be developed, under the guidance of provincial port groups. The plan should include the possibility of replacing or reusing shorelines with heavy pollution and low use. Strict approvals must be required for setting intensive utilization levels of shorelines.

A study is needed to establish a mechanism to regulate the use of shorelines; and a compensation system for the use of shoreline resources is needed to promote the economical and intensive use of shorelines. Joint supervision and management by the Ministry of Transport, the Ministry of Water Resources, and city governments are needed to fight the illegal occupation of terminal shoreline resources.

Aligning port planning with urban, waterway, and transport planning and ecological guidelines

The "Regulations on Port Planning and Management" (Ministry of Transport 2009) stipulate that port planning should conform to the plan of the urban system and be consistent with the master plan for land use, the urban master plan, the river basin plan, the flood control plan, ocean functional zoning, the waterway transport development plan, and other modes of transport. Port planning should also be coordinated with other relevant plans stipulated by laws and administrative regulations.

The development and use of port shorelines must be in line with port planning. On the basis of overall port planning and actual port development and economic development needs, port management departments should formulate integrated five-year port shoreline plans.

In 2018, the central authorities issued guidelines on the "ecological red line strategy." These guidelines call for strict enforcement of protection over certain zones. Port shoreline development and utilization activities should not threaten the safety of drinking water resources or adversely affect the ecological functions of the red line region. Functional areas should be clearly positioned in the urban development strategic plan. Based on the orientation of urban planning, the port also needs subplans for different areas, including containers, bulk, petrochemicals, grain and oil processing, and tourism. Port land use planning can be divided into port terminal transportation areas and dockside industrial parks. Dockside industrial parks can engage in equipment manufacturing; marine technology; and food processing, petrochemical, modern metallurgy, modern logistics, and other industries. Heavily polluting heavy-chemical industries must be located far away from urban areas; less-polluting light industry and high-tech industries can be located within urban areas.

Increasing the availability of anchorages

With the improvement in waterway conditions, the trend toward larger and more specialized inland vessels continues. Demand for anchorages has increased with the increase in vessel flows. Because anchorage is an important public resource, government departments will increase the number of public anchorage berths for large vessels. But integrated planning needs to be strengthened for better utilization, and management needs to be improved.

Opening new sections of the Grand Canal

The Grand Canal—the world's longest artificial waterway—has been an important waterway connecting northern China with the south since the Sui Dynasty. It is currently navigable from Jining in Shandong Province to the south. By the end of 2020, the Tongzhou section of the Grand Canal will open for navigation, providing tourist transportation and realizing the cultural belt of the Grand Canal (the cultural facilities and activities related to the Grand Canal). Resumption of navigation is also being sped up for waterways in Tianjin, Hebei, and other sections.

Accounting for all values of the waterway

Port and waterway planning follow clear sets of rules for approval. These rules could be improved by accounting for the nontransport values of the waterway in a more structured way (box 5.3). Based on the different values of the waterway, the coordinating mechanism should set priorities for the waterway and establish principles for management decisions. User requirements may change as a result of a changing society and its changing preferences. The management model has to adapt to these changes.

Shipping is just one function of a waterway (figure 5.1). In many countries, it is not the highest priority.

BOX 5.3

Multiple uses of waterways require adaptive management models

There is no commonly accepted model for integrated water management. Different countries have adopted different approaches (see box 5.4), some with more success than others. Local priorities (for example, flood prevention, irrigation, hydropower, IWT) determine the priorities and the guiding factors.

The coordinating mechanism should set priorities and establish principles for management decisions on the basis of the different values of the waterway. User requirements may change as a result of a changing society and its changing preferences. The management model has to adapt to these changes; criteria may change.

Integrated water management is more common in Europe than in China. In the Netherlands, the government manages waterways and major infrastructural facilities. It takes an integrated approach, balancing the needs of all stakeholders. The government makes the rules necessary for smooth sailing, classifying waterways, registering barges, certifying operators and crew, regulating working and resting times, standardizing navigational aids, setting speed limits, and directing upstream and downstream traffic. For all of these tasks, it generally adopts international standards, especially when waterways are navigable for seagoing or coastal shipping. The government also helps ensure fair competition by clearly defining the rights and obligations of various nautical users. When waterway use is subject to limitations, such as pollution control measures or safety requirements, the government must enforce them equally across the board.

Different models exist in other European countries. Some countries, such as Germany and most Danube countries, have more limited mandates. In others, such as Austria and France, the waterway agency has a wide mandate. In these countries, an agency covers almost all aspects of governance and development of IWT. In Austria, ViaDonau—the agency within the Austrian Ministry for Transport, Innovation, and Technology tasked with preserving and developing the Danube waterway—handles water management and river governance; substantial activity, also on the international level, is deployed in the development of IWT markets (promotion, supporting initiatives) and technological development (greening). In France, Voies Navigables de France (VNF) is responsible for the use of surface water by agriculture and industry (power plants). Unlike Germany and the Netherlands, which have IWT promotion bureaus, Austria and France have integrated promotion activities in their waterway management agencies. VNF, for example, initiated river dating, which is now common in several countries. The Compagnie National du Rhône (CNR) manages the Rhône River and the hydroelectric power plants along it. It has built and manages 18 industrial and port sites on the Rhône.

National governments do not work in isolation. The Central Commission for Navigation on the Rhine (CCNR) was created in 1815 to ensure freedom of navigation on international waterways. It has established rules that are valid across the navigable Rhine River network. These regulations—on safety, environment, labor conditions, nautical-technical aspects, hazardous substances, waste collection and processing, and social issues, for example—have long served as models for regulators elsewhere. Over the past few decades, the European Union has also issued directives on inland shipping and asked member states to apply them to their own national legislation. Most of the regulations on the Rhine and other waterways are now aligned or are being aligned under the Comité Européen pour l'Élaboration de Standards dans le Domaine de Navigation Intérieure (CESNI).

FIGURE 5.1

Different functions of waterways

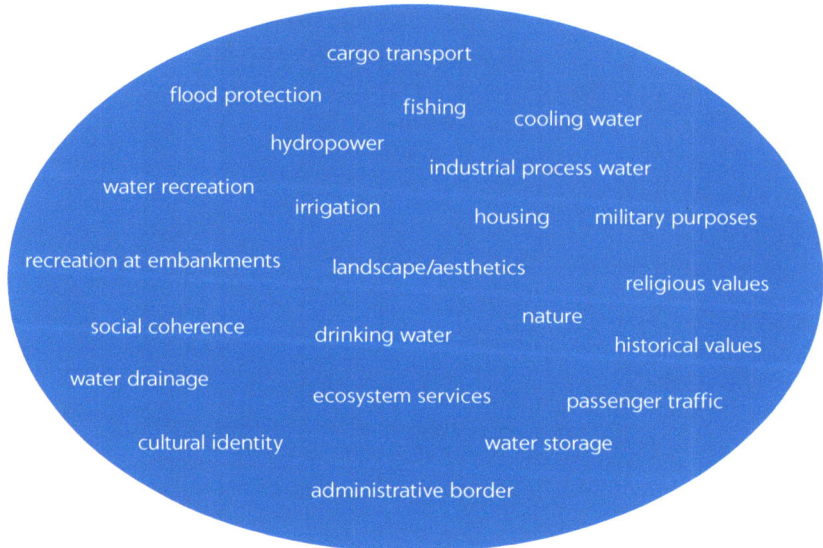

Source: PIANC WG 139 2013.

Different authorities can be engaged in the management of different aspects of waterways. A good coordination mechanism must be established to ensure that they work in concert.

To see why coordination is necessary, consider what happens during a drought. The inland shipping sector requires a minimum water level to guarantee good draft for navigation. Irrigation needs to extract more water to prevent crops from drying or dying. Hydropower facilities must safeguard a continuous flow of water through their turbines. These interests may conflict; a coordinating mechanism is required to reconcile them. In addition, the wide variations in water levels that are likely because of climate change increase the need for coordination.

As social and economic activities evolve, the uses of water and the ways in which it is valued will change (Hijdra 2017). The management bodies involved—many of them set up long ago—have their mandates from the past, even though the uses and value of the waterway have changed. The US Army Corps of Engineers, for example, was established in 1775; the Netherlands' water agency (the Rijkswaterstaat) was established in 1798; the Central Commission for Navigation on the Rhine (CCNR) was created in 1815; and the Act of Mannheim, adopted in 1848, still guides free access to the Rhine.

The uses of waterways can be classified into four categories (PIANC InCom WG 139 2016):

- Waterways as logistical corridors (for cargo transportation and passenger traffic)
- Waterways as a sociogeographic element (as sources of recreation at embankments, social coherence, religious values, housing, historical values, landscape/aesthetics, cultural identity, military purposes, and as determinants of administrative borders)

- Waterways as water resource systems (for drinking, cooling, industrial processes, irrigation, hydropower, storage, fisheries, and water management)
- Waterways as ecological systems

Improving safety

Supervision of the safe development of IWT needs strengthening. Strict examination must be conducted, and approval granted, especially for access by vessels that transport passengers or hazardous substances. Local government departments are increasing capital investment to strengthen the inland waterway rescue force, and efforts are being made to develop a plan that integrates the monitoring of safety, the navigation and emergency response, and the organization of regular search-and-rescue exercises to improve speed and efficiency in responding to accidents.

GREENING AND ADAPTION TO CLIMATE CHANGE

China is devoting increasing attention to the environmental performance of IWT and the adaptation of waterways to climate change. Actively promoting the application of new energy and clean energy will be continued and strengthened in the coming years.

To address climate change and to make the sector greener, China needs to take several steps:

- Enhance the requirements for controlling the air pollution emissions of inland vessels.
- Adjust and expand the geographical scope of the emission control areas in the Yangtze River Delta region, and enhance the requirements for control of emissions by inland vessels.
- Enhance the supervision of marine fuel quality and distribute equipment that rapidly detects the sulfur content of marine fuel distributed (or procured by) third-party testing services. In addition to implementing the plan for the established vessel emission control area, as of January 1, 2019, the sulfur content of vessels sailing into the vessel emission control area of the Yangtze River Delta shall not exceed 0.5 percent mass by mass. This standard was formulated ahead of the low-sulfur fuel standard to be formulated by the International Maritime Organization in 2020.
- Implement the construction plan for reception, transport, and disposal areas of pollutants and the layout plan for the overwater tank-cleaning stations on the Yangtze River trunk waterway.
- Promote the use of shore power by anchored ships, reduce the cost of shore power, improve the construction and utilization rate of shore power facilities, and accelerate the construction of shore power facilities at port terminals and the transformation of power-receiving facilities of vessels. Design and construct shore power facilities for new terminals according to law. By the end of 2020, full coverage of shore power will be realized at Yangtze River Delta inland ports, overwater service areas, and anchorage areas for lockage. Other inland ports will follow.
- Increase energy conservation and reduce emissions at ports, promote clean production of port facilities and equipment, and gradually eliminate and upgrade port equipment that causes high pollution and high emissions.

- Expand the green port concept to inland ports.
- Continue to actively promote the use of liquefied natural gas (LNG) and electric vessels. Local governments are encouraged to increase subsidies for the use of vessels that use new energy and clean energy and to implement incentive policies that give priority to lockage or berthing and departing. Accelerate implementation of the layout plan for LNG filling terminals along the Yangtze River trunk waterway.

Do the trends toward integrated water management, the greening of transport, and the need for climate adaptability affect the way IWT infrastructure is planned and developed? Box 5.4 describes the change in thinking.

BOX 5.4

The infrastructure dilemma: To build or not to build?

Adaptations of waterways have had both positive and negative effects on inland shipping. In several countries, other uses of the waterways—such as the generation of hydropower—were more important than shipping. They resulted in the construction of dams for hydropower generation that did not include ship locks, closing the waterway to traffic. Construction of the Itaipú Dam, on the border of Paraguay and Brazil—the second-largest dam/hydropower complex in the world after the Three Gorges Dam—put an end to international shipping on the Paraná River because a ship lock was not part of the project. At the time of construction (1971–82), IWT was not considered important because the focus had shifted to highway transport. Policy makers are now conducting a feasibility study to determine whether a ship-lock complex should be built next to the dam.

In India, a dam was constructed on the Ganges River near the border with Bangladesh. It produces thermal hydropower. The dam itself has no lock complex, but a bypass feeder canal was supposed to allow transit between Bangladesh and India. The works contained a canal and a lock, but they were not finished, and the canal is now silted. Now, traffic between north India and Bangladesh/northeast India has to follow a long route via Kolkata and the coastal route. There are plans to renovate and reopen the lock.

Balancing the interests of all stakeholders leads to a dilemma. Should infrastructure be built? Which value of waterways is most important?

Solutions are difficult because the interests of different stakeholders can conflict. In the framework of

its Trans-European Network for Transport (TEN-T) program, the European Commission developed an approach called good navigation status (GNS). It is being developed through a process of continuous improvement cycle that seeks to achieve the following attributes of integrated waterway management:

- Targeted: Every waterway maintenance or management activity should be performed within the framework of defined targets (target values, levels of service, and so forth).
- Strategic: For the coordinated, effective, and efficient achievement of targets, a specific waterway management strategy should be applied, with the goal of achieving and maintaining GNS (by no later than 2030 in the case of European waterways).
- Multidisciplinary: Waterways are not only traffic routes; they are used for a variety of other purposes, which often have conflicting interests.
- Participatory: Because of the multidisciplinary character of waterways, participatory management is advisable to understand and respect all uses of waterways. All relevant stakeholders should be engaged in the planning process to achieve and maintain GNS.

Discussions with stakeholders and waterway managers reveal that the GNS process should fulfill the following additional requirements:

- Fact-driven: The process should create transparency for all involved parties; lack of compliance with target values should be easily monitored by means of selected performance indicators.

continued

Box 5.4, *continued*

- Minimum administrative burden: The process and reporting efforts should be minimized by using data and digital sources to the maximum extent possible, possibly supported by funds from the European Commission to develop the data and interface with available databases and the legislative framework. Databases should be harmonized, and multiple requests and delivery of similar data should be avoided.

- The GNS process as a means to an end: Data collection and reporting are not goals; they are means for achieving a well-functioning waterway system in line with the provisions of relevant regulations that are verifiable by monitoring key performance indicators on the network and assessing feedback from transport users.

Several steps are needed to achieve GNS in the European Union by 2030 (figure B5.4.1).

FIGURE B.5.4.1

Next steps in the good navigation status process

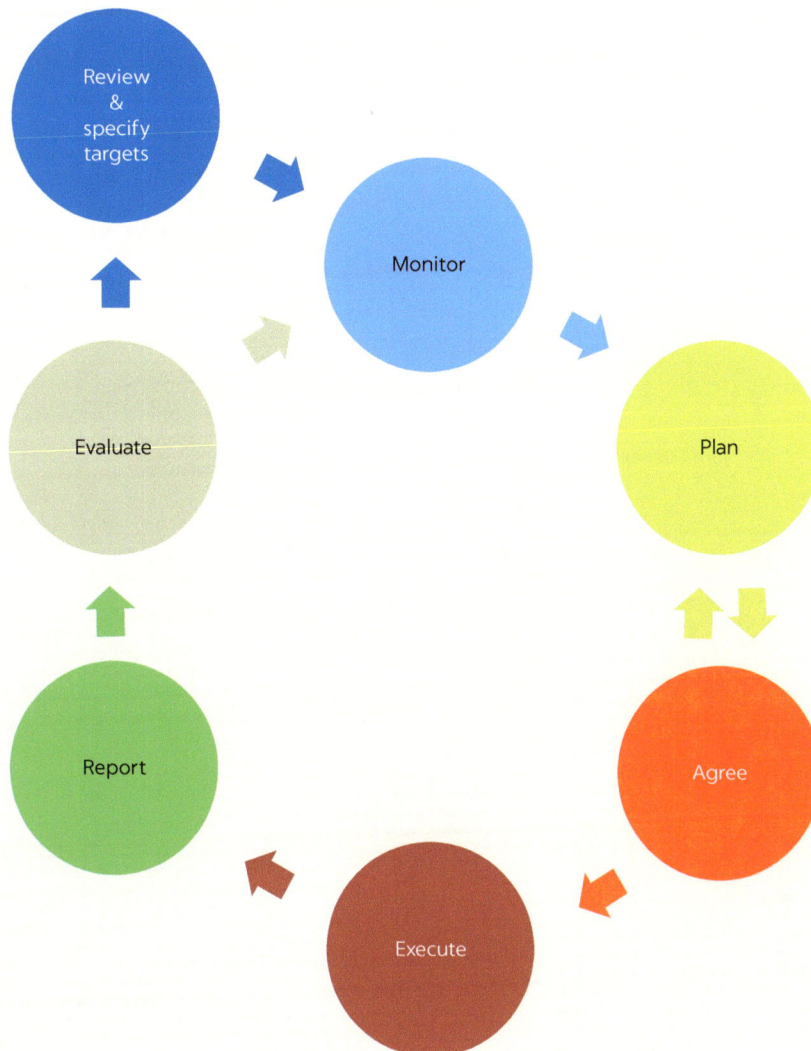

Source: Directorate-General for Mobility and Transport (European Commission) and others 2018.

Investigating alternatives to large-scale infrastructure projects

Capacity enhancement and waterway infrastructure improvements have contributed significantly to economic development in China. Every year, for example, more than 50 million tons of cargo flows in each direction through the massive ship-lock complex at the Three Gorges Dam—in 2019, the cargo flows through both directions of the Three Gorges lock and ship lift reached a record high of 148 million tons. The government's Go West policy would not have been as successful as it was without these capacity enhancements.

Dams and ship locks have been created along many waterways in China. Hydropower for navigation projects has enhanced capacity for IWT on many smaller waterways, raising the capacities for vessels on some rivers from 500 to 2,000 deadweight tons (DWT). As a result, inland ports along the waterways—such as the port of Changsha in Hunan, along the Xiang River—were able to develop container terminals.

However, large infrastructure works are no longer the preferred method for improving IWT. In 2016, in an apparent effort to breathe life into the area's heavily degraded environment, President Xi Jinping ruled out new development projects on the embattled Yangtze River. Policy had shifted: after decades of construction, environmental protection and restoration would be a "dominant focus" for the Yangtze River Economic Belt. Authorities along China's larger river were to "work together for major protection, instead of carrying out major development," as President Xi Jinping requested.

Better integration of the different values of waterways and a move toward integrated management of waterways are important elements in climate change adaptation. They become even more important with the increase in variations in water flows and water levels. Deepening of waterways, canalization, cutting of river bends for easier navigation, and other physical interventions in waterways were once the norm to enhance shipping capacity. The philosophy is now moving away from these hard interventions and toward a more adaptive approach (box 5.5).

BOX 5.5

New guiding principles for waterway interventions: Working with nature, room for the river, and aquapuncture

The World Association for Waterborne Transport Infrastructure (PIANC) has adopted "Working with Nature" (also called "Building with Nature") (PIANC 2011) as the guiding principle for waterway interventions. The principle calls for a shift in thinking in the approach to navigation development projects to help deliver mutually beneficial solutions. It promotes a proactive, integrated philosophy that focuses on achieving project objectives in an ecosystem context rather than assessing the consequences of a predefined project design. It focuses on identifying win-win solutions rather than simply minimizing ecological harm. "Working with Nature" considers project objectives from the perspective of the natural system rather than from the perspective of technical design. It does not mean that development objectives are no longer achieved. Rather, it ensures that these objectives are satisfied in a way that maximizes

continued

Box 5.5, *continued*

opportunities and reduces frustrations, delays, and extra costs (PIANC 2011).

Adopting the Working with Nature philosophy means doing things in a different order. Instead of developing a design and then assessing its environmental impacts—an approach that inevitably merely limits damage and is ultimately not sustainable—Working with Nature advocates the following steps (PIANC EnviCom WG 176 2018):

- Establish project need and objectives
- Understand the environment
- Make meaningful use of stakeholder engagement
- Identify win-win options
- Prepare project proposals/designs to benefit navigation and nature

For IWT systems, the idea was traditionally the bigger, the better. Heavy floods in Western Europe in the mid-1990s and growing concerns about the effects of climate change on water flows fostered a change in thinking. Recognizing that a new approach was needed, the Dutch Public Works Agency developed the Room for the Rivers program, consisting of hundreds of projects and interventions in different areas (figure B5.5.1).

Working with Nature and Room for the River concepts are gaining general acceptance. In some cases, these approaches take steps back toward the original flow of the waterway. They can include the removal of obstacles and the undoing of previous interventions. The principle is to minimize physical interventions and find solutions to work with waterways' natural flow as much as possible.

The Inland Waterway Authority of India (IWAI) is responsible for developing India's national waterways. In recent years, it has taken up the challenging task of redeveloping National Waterway 1, the Ganges/Hoogly River system, as a commercial waterway for freight and passengers. Studies concluded that physical adaptations had to be minimized because of environmental requirements, animal and nature conservation areas, and religious sensitivities and because the cost of deepening certain parts of the waterways would not be offset by economic benefits in terms of volume increase.

IWAI decided to follow the principle of Working with Nature. It adopted a balanced set of measures that consisted of using historical means of guiding the flow (known as *bandalling*), designing shallow draft vessels, adopting greening solutions and

FIGURE B5.5.1
Room for the river solutions

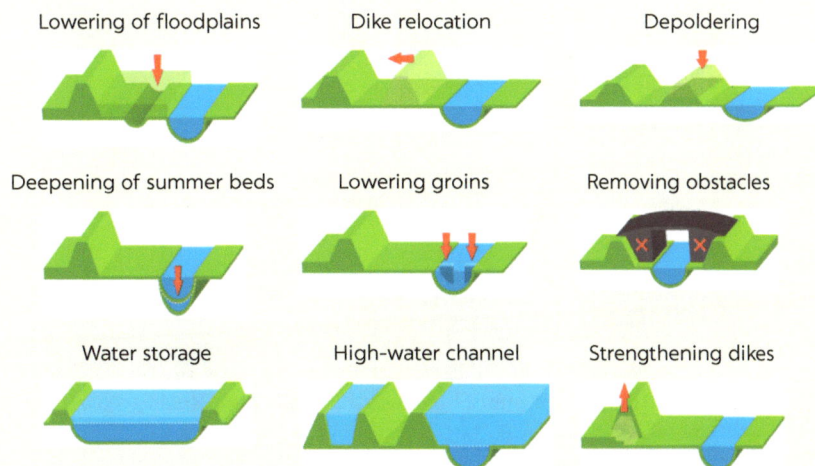

Source: Rijkswaterstaat 2016.

continued

Box 5.5, *continued*

environmental protection measures, and implementing advanced management and control. Dredging was limited to sites where interventions were absolutely necessary. IWAI is following this new approach for future waterway projects.

Aquapuncture (figure B5.5.2) reflects the same philosophy. Like acupuncture, it minimizes interventions and physical adaptations, acting only where it is absolutely necessary.

FIGURE B5.5.2

Aquapuncture: Connecting inland waterways with main port development and nature reserve areas via building with nature

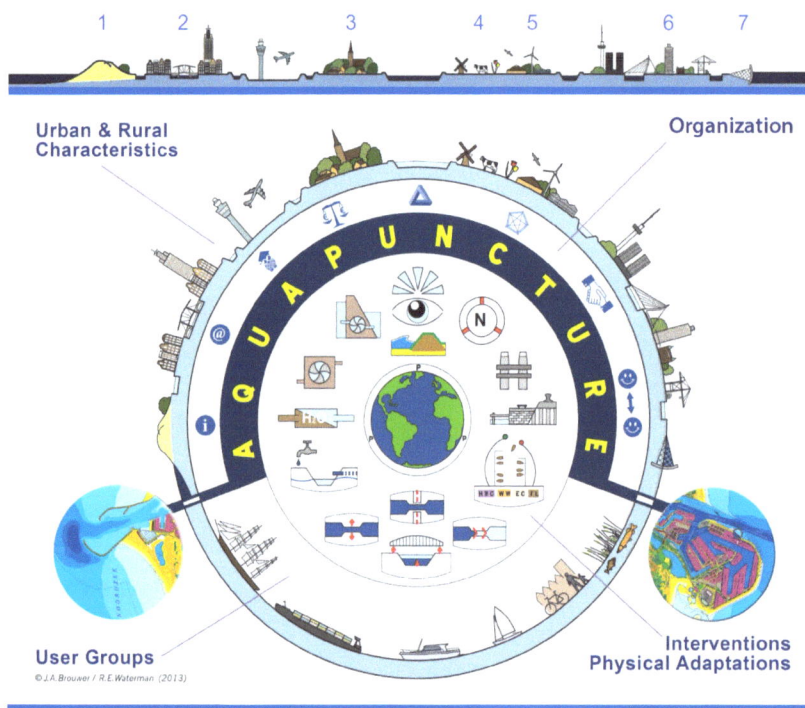

Source: Waterman and Brouwer 2015.
Note: 1 = soft coastal defense; 2 = city; 3 = village; 4 = culture and history; 5 = farms, agriculture, horticulture, nature; 6 = modern city and port; 7 = strong coastal defense.

TECHNOLOGICAL INNOVATIONS AND STANDARDIZATION

Technological innovations can contribute to the greening of waterways and the environmental protection of Yangtze River areas. They can also increase efficiency and safety and reduce operational costs.

The level of standardization and environmental performance of inland vessels must continue to be improved, and their competitiveness must be enhanced. For restricted inland waterways with navigation facilities such as ship locks and ship lifts, a series of dimension standards for navigable vessels will be formulated and enforced to improve the navigational efficiency of inland waterways and to increase the average tonnage of inland vessels. The formulation and implementation of national standards for the main dimensions of lockage vessels on the Grand Canal and the Huaihe River basin must be sped up and the optimization of vessels must be promoted.

The barge standardization of the Yangtze River and the development of river-sea transport require improved navigation capacity of the tributaries of the Yangtze River. New approaches to capacity augmentation could be studied.

A focus is now on supporting research on and the development of 124 twenty-foot equivalent unit (TEU) vessels from the river network of the Yangtze River Delta to the Yangshan Deep-Water Port and the development of river-sea vessels from the Yangtze River trunk waterway to the Yangshan Deep-Water Port and Ningbo Zhoushan Port. Efforts are also being made to promote research and development on river-sea vessels and bulk cargo ships from the main ports in the northern Jiangsu section of the Grand Canal to Lianyungang Port. The recommended route for river-sea vessels must be planned and water safety supervision must be strengthened.

Along with further standardization of the fleet, the elimination or renovation of many types of vessels has to be accelerated. The scrapping of vessels that are more than 20 years old should be encouraged. Also, inland vessels with high emissions must be restricted or banned. The application of LNG and other clean energy vessels in IWT should be promoted. Standardization is important to facilitate large-scale application.

Advanced technological means—such as electronic navigation channel charts, additional river information services (RIS) applications, and e-tools—can be used to improve the organizational efficiency of IWT and promote the transport of high-value cargoes on waterways.

MULTIMODAL CONNECTIVITY

Ongoing demonstration projects in China include combined container sea-rail transport projects at ports along the Yangtze River, multimodal steel transport projects in Ma'anshan, and other projects, as well as the swap trailer combined highway-railway transport project of the Three Gorges Dam. The goal of these projects is to demonstrate the advantages of multimodal transport. They will show where transport infrastructure should be adjusted and optimized to increase efficiency and reduce logistics costs. Bottlenecks restricting the development of multimodal transport should gradually be removed to improve the quality and level of multimodal transport services.

The development and promotion of multimodal transport and the consolidation and status-raising of regional multimodal transport centers require continued attention. Existing railway logistics bases, highway ports, and inland ports are a good basis for stimulating construction of freight hubs (logistics parks) that serve multimodal transport and connect trunk and branch lines. Areas that may need support include the construction of access railways and yard stations for inland ports.

This study was not able to determine the bottlenecks that are preventing logistics enterprises from setting up integrated logistics services. The management model of ports/terminals and water/rail services, which restricts third parties from setting up these types of services, may be hampering integration into supply chains.

Further integration of IWT in supply chains and in multimodal transport will result in a larger catchment area for water transport, as illustrated in box 5.6.

BOX 5.6

Integration of inland waterway transport in multimodal supply chains

In the single-mode system, IWT reduces costs when pre- and end-haul transport—the so-called last mile transport—is limited and the trunk transport exceeds a certain distance. Modern IWT operations with new and innovative vessels that are integrated in supply chains and multimodal systems lead to even more efficient operations, reducing logistics costs and consequently the break-even distance (table B5.6.1).

The influence area of a waterway often is regarded as a fixed distance from the waterway. In fact, it varies, based on several criteria, especially in integrated multimodal systems. The main criterion is the direction of the trunk line and the pre- or end-haul transport.

When they run in opposite directions, the influence area is small; when they run in the same direction, the influence area is larger. In Europe, for example, cargoes can be transported on a vessel from Rotterdam to Duisburg (200 kilometers) and continue by rail for another 500 kilometers or more (figure B5.6.1). Multimodal transport in the Yangtze basin will ideally combine east-west flows on water and north-south extensions by rail.

In figure B5.6.1, the dark blue line is the trunk line. The red line is the hinterland connection, and the blue oval shows the influence area from a node (port) when cargo moves from left to right.

TABLE B5.6.1 **Break-even distance in inland waterway transport in the Netherlands**

TYPE OF TRANSPORT	CONTAINERIZED CARGO (KILOMETERS)	DRY AND LIQUID BULK CARGO (KILOMETERS)
Wet link	20–40	20–40
Pre- or end-haul	60–100	80–120
Pre- and end-haul transport	225-250	180-200

Source: Panteia/NEA 2015.

FIGURE B5.6.1

Influence area of inland waterway transport

Source: STC-NESTRA data.

SMART INLAND SHIPPING

Improved information and communication technology can help make waterway infrastructure and ports smarter and allow IWT to provide additional services that can make operations more efficient. It also creates possibilities for applications such as autonomous shipping and automated handling.

Smart technology has affected almost all components of the production of transport and of services in general. It is expected to affect shipping in the following ways:

- Smart technologies improve the management of waterway infrastructure and navigational environment. Establishment of RIS is an important first step in the process of making infrastructure smart. A basic RIS provides information about navigation conditions (maps and positioning, waterway dimensions, current speeds). The ship operator provides information about the ship, cargo (particularly hazardous cargo), and crew. The next step for infrastructure management will be to use real-time and in-advance data from ships and infrastructure to proactively manage traffic. Such management could include optimized lock and bridge operations, berth allocations, and water depth forecasts, for example.
- Eventually, ships will be equipped with automated systems that use (external) data to optimize key functions (managing fuel consumption, monitoring and responding to the navigational environment, planning in real time). Existing vessels already have increased levels of digital support and automation. Eventually, vessels may become autonomous.
- Smart regulation and facilitation refers to the interaction between ships and government agencies for regulation or inspection. It can include information about compliance with staffing requirements or emission standards.
- Smart technology can improve communication between actors (ships, infrastructure managers, logistics parties) on booking, operational planning, invoicing, and cargo monitoring, for example. Smart communication can connect infrastructure management and ship operations with the business environment of clients (shipping lines, shippers, logistics service providers), creating opportunities for better-integrated logistics planning and operation and for reduced transaction costs.

China has begun several initiatives to accelerate the development of smart shipping:

1. It is exploring the use of artificial intelligence to replace some components and activities of inland vessels. Smart shipping can reduce vessel manning while ensuring the safety of vessel operations.
2. It is exploring the development of fully automatic and semiautomatic terminals at selected inland ports and the transformation of existing terminals using smart technology.
3. It is introducing satellite remote sensing and telemetry, big data, cloud platforms, and drones and innovative means to monitor the construction and operation of illegal terminals. Information-based means could be used to improve dispatching efficiency.

4. It is using advanced information technologies to improve the response to accidents.

5. A comprehensive information service system needs to be created, including electronic navigation channel charts of all river basins, as the basic geographic information platform. Such a system would provide information resources on all river basins that could be used in e-government, public services, e-commerce, safety supervision, logistics services, and business operations.

The application of information technology in IWT will continuously be promoted. It will include improved installation and use rates of automatic identification system (AIS) equipment for inland vessels and higher penetration of the BeiDou Navigation Satellite System in inland vessels. The application of advanced technologies such as the Internet of Things, blockchain, big data, and cloud computing in inland vessels supports the possibility to introduce corridor management on waterways. Acceleration support may be needed.

In May 2019, China issued an Intelligent Shipping Development Guideline that was jointly developed by seven ministries; it identified a long-term development plan that applies the new technologies to shipping—the first such structured approach in the world. These applications could include demonstrations of autonomous sailing, vessel platooning, construction of automated vessels and equipment, and a governance system. Smart shipping is receiving growing attention in other waterway basins, too, notably in the European Union (box 5.7).

Autonomous shipping can be considered an extreme form of smart shipping. It will be developed in stages, from assistance to full automation (table 5.1).

BOX 5.7

Smart and connected shipping in the European Union

The European Union has launched several projects and initiatives to develop smart and connected IWT. The Digital Inland Waterway Area (DINA) and the Digital Multimodal Nodes (DMN) projects address technical, legal, and economic aspects of IWT. They explore how digitization can contribute to efficient and smooth navigation and integrate IWT with other modes to optimize supply chains. Providing relevant data to stakeholders in the chain can lead to the optimization of logistics and administrative processes and reduce logistics costs.

Much still needs to be done to move from current river information services to an optimal digital environment (data platform) to allow for barge operators to control data on their vessel, voyages, cargo, and crew for their own purposes (smart navigation) and for controlled sharing with other actors (for reporting purposes, for example). A new on-board toolkit will be needed that connects barges with this digital environment and provides functionality for skippers (among other end users). Adequate governance mechanisms need to be created to develop and maintain the standards used in DINA.

Much research is ongoing in the European Union in the field of autonomous sailing, all of it in an initial phase and fragmented. Developments are expected to have a major influence on IWT. International cooperation, especially with respect to standardization and harmonization of protocols, is required.

TABLE 5.1 **Levels of automation in inland waterway transport**

	Level	Designation	Vessel command (steering, propulsion, wheelhouse, ...)	Monitoring of and responding to navigational environment	Fallback performance of dynamic navigation tasks	Remote control
Boatmaster performs part or all of the dynamic navigation tasks	0	**NO AUTOMATION** The full-time performance by the human boatmaster of all aspects of the dynamic navigation tasks, even when supported by warning or intervention systems *E.g., navigation with support of radar installation*				No
	1	**STEERING ASSISTANCE** The context-specific performance by a steering automation system using certain information about the navigational environment and with the expectation that the human boatmaster performs all remaining aspects of the dynamic navigation tasks *E.g., rate of turn regulator* *E.g., trackpilot (track-keeping system for inland vessels along predefined guidelines)*				
	2	**PARTIAL AUTOMATION** The context-specific performance by a navigation automation system of both steering and propulsion using certain information about the navigational environment and with the expectation that the human boatmaster performs all remaining aspects of the dynamic navigation tasks				
System performs all the dynamic navigation tasks (when engaged)	3	**CONDITIONAL AUTOMATION** The sustained context-specific performance by a navigation automation system of all dynamic navigation tasks, including collision avoidance, with the expectation that the human boatmaster will be receptive to requests to intervene and to system failures and will respond appropriately				Subject to context specific execution, remote control is possible (vessel command, monitoring of and responding to navigational environment and fallback performance). It may have an influence on crew requirements (number or qualification).
	4	**HIGH AUTOMATION** The sustained context-specific performance by a navigation automation system of all dynamic navigation tasks and fallback performance, without expecting a human boatmaster responding to a request to intervene[a] *E.g., vessel operating on a canal section between two successive locks (environment well known), but the automation system is not able to manage alone the passage through the lock (requiring human intervention)*				
	5	**AUTONOMOUS = FULL AUTOMATION** The sustained and unconditional performance by a navigation automation system of all dynamic navigation tasks and fallback performance, without expecting a human boatmaster to respond to a request to intervene				

Source: CCNR 2018.

a. This level introduces two different functionalities: the ability of "normal" operation without expecting human intervention, and the exhaustive fallback performance two sublevels could be envisaged.

AREAS FOR CONTINUED INTERNATIONAL COOPERATION

International institutions and development partners have supported IWT development in China and international cooperation in the field. The focus in the early years was mainly on infrastructure development. It later shifted toward support systems for traffic guidance, safety, and waste management.

Recently, emphasis has been on greening and improving environmental performance. Also, projects have been carried out in developing ports in combination with logistics zones.

There is a continued need for international cooperation and donor involvement. Involvement should focus on introducing and implementing new philosophies and new technologies that lead to a more sustainable transport system and better climate change adaptability. There is a need to support other countries in the field of IWT by sharing and applying the experiences of China and waterway basins in other countries that engage in good practices. Priority areas are described in the following subsections.

Planning and management of waterways

The coordinating mechanism for a waterway should set priorities and identify the principles for management decisions. The management model must adapt to changing user requirements as a result of a changing society and its changing preferences. Increasingly, new concepts, such as Working/Building with Nature, are being accepted throughout the different waterway basins but have yet to be widely applied in China. The GNS concept is a first step toward a more balanced decision system in water management that takes account of the needs of the inland shipping sector.

A project making use of these new concepts could demonstrate the added value for IWT development in China. It could serve as an international show-case. The World Bank could use the results of such a demonstration project as an example to be applied in other water basins.

Smart shipping

China is leading the development of intelligent and autonomous shipping, which could become an industry changer. It is the first country to set up a large-scale research and pilot project, including the assignment of a large test area.

It is important that international standards be developed in technologies, data standards, security issues, and related areas. The World Bank could play a role in this process, acting as a bridge to international application and standardization.

Enhancement of the role of small and medium enterprises in inland waterway transport

Small and medium enterprises that want to enter the IWT sector face high entrance barriers because of the substantial investment required, the long lifetime of the assets, the organizational structure, and difficulty in obtaining financing. For all of these reasons, choosing truck transport is often an easier choice. Exploiting significant market potential may require new approaches. Lessons learned in China could be applied in other countries.

Innovations related to green and sustainable inland waterway transport

China has invested heavily in LNG transport, but market breakthrough has not yet been realized. Pilots have shown that LNG is not an alternative for the entire fleet, but it offers advantages in specific cases, depending on vessel size and type of operations. Although China is promoting the use of LNG, it is not clear whether LNG is a solution for the future or should be considered more as a transition fuel, needed while alternative systems are being developed. Other fuel systems—such as fuel cells or hydrogen, solar, or full electric solutions—have potential but they are not yet ready for large scale introduction. Research is ongoing, but many technological and market challenges exist. Results achieved in the large Chinese market could provide guidance for other waterway basins.

Knowledge exchange and support system

Around the world, IWT is experiencing a revival. But no mechanism is available through which waterway authorities, government agencies, shipping companies, and shippers can easily access information in the field. Some international organizations provide this function in specific areas, such as infrastructure (the World Association for Waterborne Transport Infrastructure [PIANC]) and human resources and training (the Educational Network of Inland Navigation Schools and Training Institutes [EDINNA]), but no platform provides full coverage of all issues (policy and strategy, institutional organization, infrastructure, economics, sustainability, vessel technology, operations, information and communications technology, ports and terminals, and so forth). Where reports are available, many are in local languages (Chinese, Dutch, French, German); very little of the literature is available in English, limiting access. The information used in this report, for example, is unknown outside of China because most of it is in Chinese.

A (virtual) knowledge exchange center, initiated by the World Bank—where information about several areas in the field of IWT would be made available to organizations, countries, and companies—would greatly contribute to the dissemination of lessons and experiences in developing IWT systems. Beyond providing information, it could provide expert support in interpreting questions, help users find answers, and guide further analysis.

Transboundary dialogue about integrated waterway management can provide a good (first) opportunity to disseminate Chinese practices and lessons learned in Southeast Asia (in the Brahmaputra basin [China, Bangladesh, Vietnam] and the Mekong basin [Vietnam, Cambodia, Lao People's Democratic Republic, Myanmar, China], for example).

HIGHLIGHTS

- The development of IWT as a green, safe, and sustainable mode of transport is a continued priority. Technological innovation in the IWT sector is necessary for climate change adaptability, and new concepts like Working with Nature, in which all values and multiple use of the waterways are considered, will change how waterways are developed.
- The role of IWT can be expanded and its influence area enlarged through better multimodal connectivity.
- A better market penetration of IWT requires a market observation system, promotional mechanisms, an increased role of SMEs, and opening of the IWT system for new business solutions and different supply chains.

- Smart shipping is a technical innovation that has the potential to greatly influence the IWT sector; important in this field is international cooperation and standardization.
- A knowledge exchange mechanism will help other countries benefit from China's experiences.

REFERENCES

Chinese Policy Documents

Ministry of Transport. 2009. "Regulations on Port Planning and Management."

Ministry of Transport, Cyberspace Administration of China, National Development and Reform Committee, Ministry of Education, Ministry of Science and Technology, Ministry of Industry and Information Technology, and Ministry of Finance. 2019. "Guideline of Intelligent Shipping Development."

State Council. 2006. "Decision of the State Council on Strengthening Energy Conservation."

Other References

CCNR (Central Commission for Navigation on the Rhine). 2018. "First International Definition of Levels of Automation in Inland Navigation." Strasbourg.

Changjiang River Administration of Navigational Affairs. 2019. "Annual Report of Yangtze Navigation Authority." https://cjhy.mot.gov.cn/hydt/zhxw/201912/t20191231_151740.shtml.

Chongqing Communications Planning Survey and Design Institute. 2015. "Strategy for Restructuring Inland Waterway Transport and Multimodal Logistics in Chongqing." Chongqing.

Directorate-General for Mobility and Transport (European Commission) and TNO. 2017. "Towards a Digital Inland Waterway Area and Digital Multimodal Nodes: Waterborne Digital Services Between Maritime and Inland Ports." Luxembourg: Publications Office of the European Union.

Directorate-General for Mobility and Transport (European Commission), Inland Navigation Europe, STC-NESTRA, ViaDonau, and Vlaamse Overheid. 2018. "Guidelines Towards Achieving a Good Navigation Status." Luxembourg: Publications Office of the European Union.

Hijdra, A. 2017. "Waterways—Ways of Value: Planning for Redevelopment of an Ageing System in Modern Society." Groningen: Rijksuniversiteit Groningen.

Ministry of Transport. 2019. "Annual Report of China's Registered Crew Development 2018." Press Office of Ministry of Transport, China.

Panteia/NEA. 2015. Platina 2—Deliverable 1.6: Macro analysis of market potential. Zoetermeer.

PIANC (World Association for Waterborne Transport Infrastructure). 2011. "Working with Nature." Position Paper. Brussels.

PIANC WG 139. 2013. "Different Uses of the Waterways." Presented at SMART Rivers International Conference. Liège.

PIANC InCom WG 139. 2016. "Values of Inland Waterways." Brussels.

PIANC EnviCom WG 176. 2018. "Guide for Applying Working with Nature to Navigation Infrastructure Projects." Brussels.

Rijkswaterstaat. 2016. Dutch Water Program Room for the River factsheet. https://www.rijkswaterstaat.nl/english/water/water-safety/room-for-the-rivers/index.aspx.

Waterman, R., and J. Brouwer. 2015. "Aquapuncture: Sustainable Future of Inland Waterways." Delft. http://www.ronaldwaterman.com/page3/files/article-aquapuncture-sustainable-future-of-inland-waterways-terra-et-aqua-140-1.pdf.

6 Lessons Learned and Good Practices

Unlike the Mississippi River, the Rhine, and the Mekong, which have continuously served as commercial waterways, Chinese waterways lost their major cargo-carrying function to rail and truck transport during the 20th century. The inland waterway transport (IWT) sector has declined in several of the world's largest rivers, including the Nile, the Amazon, the Ganges, and the Volga. Less and less freight is moved by IWT, and fewer passengers consider IWT a viable alternative mode. In some countries and regions (for example, Bangladesh and Northeast India), system modernization and upgrading have not occurred. A casualty of these developments is the loss of knowledge and expertise in IWT in many emerging economies. Many policy makers are not aware of the potential of IWT or of the contribution it can make to sustainable transport systems. Many cargo owners and transport and logistics companies are not aware of the logistics advantages IWT offers or of the possibilities for IWT to fit into modern supply chains. Recently, however, changes in the global economy and the realities of climate change have refocused attention on the potential of IWT. The challenge now is that there are few examples of the potential of IWT and of how to revive it.

China's IWT system is still evolving. Its current IWT policies are grappling with improving its environmental performance, increasing multimodal connectivity, creating logistic zones along waterways, and enhancing human resources. However, much can be learned from China's experience to date. Overall, the success of its remarkable IWT development has been possible largely because of strong, sustained, and adaptable government policy. Thanks to the policy attention by Chinese leaders at all levels of government, a once-dormant IWT system is now a vibrant mode of transport in China. Indeed, the Yangtze River is now the busiest waterway in the world.

China's IWT story shows that with dedicated policies and targeted funding, inland waterway networks can be revived. However, China's IWT development is not a blueprint for others—China has a unique governance mechanism and has had unusual circumstances that may not be typical. The development of IWT in China required regular policy adjustments and testing, through a system of trial and error, with feedback loops used, and through demonstration projects of new approaches. The 16 policies presented earlier illustrate that institutional reform is not straightforward, and that in China, reforms and policy changes were not made in a sequential and neat manner.

Over the years, the focus of policy and reforms has shifted, in response to changing economic policies, insights, and societal demands. The way that China developed its IWT yields valuable lessons for other countries and river basins. However, not all experiences from China can be replicated. The trial-and-error system used in China is supported by a large and growing transport market and by a period of 10–12 percent year-on-year economic growth that justifies the risk of potential higher cost related to retrofitting the IWT system to adapt for more efficient solutions. In considering the need for the sustainable financing of infrastructure, the trial-and-error system might not be the most efficient approach for the development of other waterway systems, and it may be an impossibility for many emerging markets. The political, social, and economic contexts vary in each country. However, many countries are keen to understand how to replicate China's achievement in reviving IWT and what lessons may be drawn from its experience.

STRONG AND SUSTAINED POLICY WITH COORDINATED CENTRAL PLANNING

The experience of reviving IWT in China demonstrates the importance of strong and sustained policy coupled with coordinated central planning and support systems. The establishment of five-year development plans, in which clear and tangible goals were set by the National Development and Reform Commission, was key to successfully reviving IWT in China. And the five-year development plans were supported by policies and directives that built confidence in the sector. Fundamentally, the principal contradiction in IWT was reflected in the weak foundation of infrastructure, the historical shortage of capital construction, and the failure of transport capacity to grow rapidly enough to meet the needs of economic and social development.

During the 40 years of reforms and opening up of the IWT sector, the clear, central vision of providing safe, convenient, and efficient transport to contribute to the development of China was embedded in the various five-year plans and progressively developed. Throughout the 40-year period, IWT enjoyed prominence in China's transport policy and was linked to national goals. A series of policy guidelines and implementation plans were issued to stimulate specific development in IWT. It is significant that the five-year development plans were not a wish list of bygone eras. Each target for progressively developing the elements of IWT has been rigorously monitored, and achievements have been rewarded.

China's large population and its demand for a mass transport system greatly facilitated the development of many economic and industrial areas, such as those at the middle and upper reaches of the Yangtze River. The location of inland economic areas along waterways is an important element in attracting more cargo to waterways because it reduces pre- and end-haul transport by road—so-called last-mile connectivity.

PUBLIC SECTOR FUNDING

When the goal to revive IWT in China was set, the sector had more or less collapsed. Because of this collapse, central government policies to revive the

IWT sector were accompanied by government funding for basic infrastructure such as waterways and ports, along with associated systems, including river information services, information and communication technology (ICT), and emergency response. Targeted funding was made available when specific measures and actions were needed and when the sector needed support. For example, as part of the barge standardization program, funds were provided for scrapping old vessels. Funding came from various sources, including government budgets, construction surcharges, and specially created IWT funds. Several provinces set up additional funding schemes. In addition, funding is available for demonstration projects that test new solutions, applications, and innovations.

In the parts of the IWT sector that generally would be considered to be part of the private sector in Europe and the United States, those areas of the IWT sector also benefited from public funding. For example, as a result of several years of neglect, the barriers to entry for operators were high and commercial banks found the sector extremely risky. Thus, from a messaging perspective, but also from initial experimentation with funding the sector, China provided the resources to develop core infrastructure but also to de-risk and encourage alternative investments. Transforming a rigid, planned economic system into a unified, open, and competitive IWT market required an enormous change in mind-set. Leaders at all levels of the IWT industry made bold innovations and focused on solving deeply rooted problems in the sector. China opened up to foreign technologies, capital, and management experience, and state financing was replaced by a diversified investment and financing climate.

Today, different financing mechanisms are in existence worldwide to cover part of the operational costs for waterway managers, and good practices in public-private partnership contracts have been developed (for example, performance-based contracts for dredging, concession models for waterway management, and infrastructure for inland ports and terminals). However, public investment is needed to revive and develop IWT infrastructure and operations, especially in low-income countries and in countries in the initial stages of development. For new IWT projects, the process of impact assessment and evaluation should consider wider benefits in terms of economic, social, and environmental performance, instead of conventional cost-benefit analysis because inland waterways have an effect on hinterlands and other areas.

STRENGTHENING INSTITUTIONS AND COORDINATED DEVELOPMENT OF INLAND WATERWAY TRANSPORT

The coordination of different parties involved in the development of IWT has been a major factor in the sector's success. Since reform and opening up, the combination of central and regional systems, the distribution of responsibilities at different levels, and joint construction have created a framework for accelerating the development of inland waterway infrastructure. The Ministry of Transport and local governments jointly constructed inland ports and waterways. Under the coordination of the central government, China established coordination platforms and created partnerships between and within the provinces and cities along the Yangtze River, jointly promoting the development of the Yangtze River Golden Waterway. By constantly deepening efforts, major reforms in the management structure of IWT and the port management system of the Yangtze River have been realized. By continuing to strengthen and improve industrial management and constantly exploring and innovating the scope, content, means, and methods of inland waterway management under market economy conditions, China has created a favorable environment for IWT development.

SYNCHRONIZATION OF IMPROVEMENT OF INFRASTRUCTURE, STANDARDIZATION OF VESSELS, AND CLASSIFICATION OF WATERWAYS

Unlike many countries that take a piecemeal approach to developing aspects of IWT, China learned early on from the experience in Europe and the United States that the entire ecosystem of IWT must be developed in tandem to achieve long-term goals. The sustainable, rapid, and sound development of inland waterways requires scientific development strategies, long-term plans, and phased objectives. Since reform and opening up, the IWT industry has implemented a step-by-step reform and improvement program that reflects China's changing national planning and development principles, guided by the policies issued by the central government and by several key policy documents. The step-by-step approach began with infrastructure improvements and upgrading, followed by fleet improvements and standardization, and the opening up of the market for private business and the decoupling of government and enterprise activities. Its focus then shifted to quality improvements. Local governments followed the centrally guided approach by setting up waterway programs in their provinces. Through State Council documents, IWT has become a national priority, as illustrated by the implementation of the Yangtze River Economic Belt and the Xijiang River Economic Belt and the movement of IWT into a new period of important strategic opportunities.

Much attention was given to the societal advantages of IWT, and a sharper focus was put on the further greening of the IWT system. After policy makers concluded that standardization of facilities and equipment was needed, China established standardization guidelines. Standardization of waterways was a first important step in developing an approach that could be applied on a wider scale. The classification of waterways defined waterway standards and dimensions and made a vessel classification and standardization program possible. The barge standardization program led to an upgrading of the fleet and the removal of old, polluting, and unsafe vessels from the market. It had a major effect on vessel quality and size, resulting in better economic, safety, and environmental performance. Green ports, green vessels, and efficiency improvements through ICT applications are examples of China's proactive approach. China has invested and heavily supports the development of liquefied natural gas (LNG) vessels, despite the technological challenges and the uncertainties about the effects on operational costs. The United States and the countries along the Rhine River shared similar policy goals but failed to realize a breakthrough. China has realized a substantial shift to LNG, but pilot projects have shown that LNG is a solution for only part of the fleet. Therefore, China is investigating new energy sources for inland shipping and has become a leader in this field. Thanks to the size of its fleet and its IWT system, China enjoys economies of scale that make investments pay off more quickly than in other countries.

DEDICATED EDUCATIONAL SYSTEM FOR IWT IS NEEDED TO REVIVE THE SECTOR

China developed a system for training and educating people to work in the IWT sector—at vocational training centers, shipping colleges, and universities—that is based on standardized qualification and certification requirements. It also created research institutes in the sector. In addition to investing in infrastructure and related policies, China established the full spectrum of IWT-related education, and it is the only country in the world to have established inland shipping universities. In other countries, IWT personnel are educated in vocational schools and IWT professions cannot generally achieve academic qualifications in the sector. Also, China has established many shipping colleges and schools that provide training at all levels. The curriculum has been continuously upgraded. Because of the modernization of the sector and upgrading of vessels and equipment, the adoption of new technologies (ICT), and the handling of hazardous cargoes, ever-increasing skills are required by the staff and crews of inland shipping companies. Reforms in the educational system were needed to meet these growing demands.

HIGHLIGHTS

- The experience of developing IWT in China reveals that the barriers to developing IWT after a long period of underinvestment and neglect can be overcome. However, a long-term horizon is needed to develop or revive IWT. China's economy and society are now heavily dependent on the proper functioning of the IWT system.
- China's experience is not a blueprint; China has a unique governance mechanism and has had an unusual set of circumstances that may not be typical. The political, social, and economic contexts vary in each country. However, many countries are keen to understand how to replicate China's achievement in reviving IWT and what lessons may be drawn from its experience.
- For new IWT projects, the process of impact assessment and evaluation should consider wider benefits in terms of economic, social, and environmental performance.
- The lessons learned in China are valuable for other countries that are developing or redeveloping an IWT system.
- A strong and sustained policy, coupled with coordinated central planning, is required.
- Public sector funding after several years of noninvestment is inevitable, especially during nascent stages.
- The strengthening of institutions and a coordinated development of IWT is required.
- The improvement of infrastructure and fairways, the standardization of vessels, and the classification of waterways must be synchronized.
- A dedicated educational system for all aspects of IWT is needed to revive the sector.

Major Inland Ports in China

Source: World Bank map IBRD 45271, August 2020.

According to the Port Law of China, in 2004, 28 inland ports were categorized as major inland ports.

Yangtze River basin (15 major ports)

Luzhou

Chongqing

Yichang

Jingzhou

Wuhan

Huangshi

Changsha

Yueyang

Nanchang

Jiujiang

Wuhu

Anqing

Maanshan

Hefei

Wuxi

Pearl River basin (5 ports)

Nanning

Guigang

Wuzhou

Zhaoqing

Foshan

Grand Canal and Huaihe River basin (6 ports)

Jining

Xuzhou

Bengbu

Hangzhou

Jiaxing

Huzhou

Heilongjiang River system and Songliao River basin (2 ports)

Harbin

Kiamusze

www.ingramcontent.com/pod-product-compliance
Lightning Source LLC
Chambersburg PA
CBHW041445210326
41599CB00004B/135